Praise for God's Gl

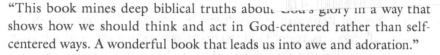

"This book mines deep biblical truths about ⌐od, glory in a way that shows how we should think and act in God-centered rather than self-centered ways. A wonderful book that leads us into awe and adoration."

—DAVID F. WELLS, Distinguished Research Professor, Gordon-Conwell Theological Seminary

"Between these covers, one of our day's most thoughtful and prolific Reformed thinkers serves up a robust and edifying exposition of the cardinal cry of the Reformed tradition, *soli Deo gloria*. As VanDrunen deftly demonstrates, this "sola" is no ordinary slogan; everything turns on what these three little words declare and his God-centered and Christ-focused treatment draws out the heart of Scripture, through the Reformed tradition, and applies it directly to our ever too vanity-distracted lives. Take this book up; it will do you much good."

—BRUCE P. BAUGUS, Associate Professor of Philosophy and Theology, Reformed Theological Seminary

"The solas of the Reformation too easily devolve into empty slogans. David VanDrunen's book is a precious remedy against such devolution. VanDrunen traces the radiant arc of God's glory from its internal fullness in the blessed Trinity to its external manifestation in creation and covenant, in the triune work of salvation, and in God's eternal kingdom. Along the way, he addresses the vices that inhibit us from admiring and answering God's glory and provides practical instruction in the virtues that promote awe and adoration in the presence of our glorious God. Reading this book will reinvigorate wonder and worship to the glory of God alone."

—SCOTT R. SWAIN, Professor of Systematic Theology and Academic Dean at Reformed Theological Seminary, Orlando

"This book does much more than defend a reformation slogan. VanDrunen's examination of *soli Deo gloria* explores who God is and who God intends us to be. Clearly and occasionally wonderfully written, thorough, wise, and biblically deep, it says so much that Christians in our day should hear that I find myself picturing venues—Sunday School, student discussion groups, class assignments—where I can use it. Read it and grow."

—MARK R. TALBOT, Associate Professor of Philosophy, Wheaton College

Praise for the Five Solas Series

"The Protestant Reformation was driven by a renewed appreciation of the singular fullness of the triune God and his unique sovereignty in all of human life. But that profound reality expressed itself with regard to many questions and in a number of forms, ranging from facets of the liturgy to soteriological tenets and back again. I'm delighted to see this new series expositing the five most influential expressions of that God-centeredness, the pivotal *solas* of the Protestant Reformation. By expounding the biblical reasoning behind them, I hope these volumes will invigorate a more profoundly theological vision of our lives and callings as Christians and churches."

—MICHAEL ALLEN, Associate Professor of Systematic and Historical Theology, Reformed Theological Seminary

"The Reformation's 500th Anniversary will be celebrated as a significant historical event. However, The Five Solas series explores the contemporary relevance of this legacy for the global church. Superb evangelical scholars have been enlisted not only to summarize the 'solas,' but to engage each from historical, exegetical, and constructive perspectives. These volumes demonstrate that, far from being exhausted slogans, the Reformation's key themes need to be rediscovered for the church's very existence and mission in the world."

—MICHAEL HORTON, J. Gresham Machen Professor of Systematic Theology and Apologetics, Westminster Seminary California

"I welcome this new series and its substantial engagement with the great themes of Reformation theology."

—TIMOTHY GEORGE, founding dean of Beeson Divinity School of Samford University and general editor of the *Reformation Commentary on Scripture*.

"A timely project, and not simply because the 500th anniversary of the Reformation will soon be upon us. Much of 'who we are' is determined by "where we have come from"; at a time when even so significant a part of our past as the Reformation is, for many, little more than a name, informed, accessible treatments of its basic principles are welcome indeed."

—STEPHEN WESTERHOLM, Professor of Early Christianity, McMaster University

God's Glory
ALONE

THE MAJESTIC HEART OF
CHRISTIAN FAITH AND LIFE

The Five Solas Series

Edited by Matthew Barrett

Books in Series:

God's Word Alone—The Authority of Scripture
  by Matthew M. Barrett

Christ Alone—The Uniqueness of Jesus as Savior
  by Stephen J. Wellum

Grace Alone—Salvation as a Gift of God
  by Carl R. Trueman

Faith Alone—The Doctrine of Justification
  by Thomas R. Schreiner

*God's Glory Alone—The Majestic Heart of
  Christian Faith and Life*
  by David VanDrunen

THE **5 SOLAS** SERIES

God's Glory
ALONE

THE MAJESTIC HEART OF
CHRISTIAN FAITH AND LIFE

What the Reformers Taught
. . . and Why It Still Matters

DAVID VANDRUNEN

MATTHEW BARRETT, SERIES EDITOR

ZONDERVAN

God's Glory Alone — The Majestic Heart of Chrisitan Faith and Life
Copyright © 2015 by David VanDrunen

This title is also available as a Zondervan ebook. Visit www.zondervan.com/ebook

Requests for information should be addressed to:
Zondervan, 3900 *Sparks Dr. SE, Grand Rapids, Michigan 49546*

Library of Congress Cataloging-in-Publication Data

VanDrunen, David, 1971-
    God's glory alone—the majestic heart of Christian faith and life: what the reformers
taught . . . and why it still matters / David VanDrunen.
      192 pages   cm.—(The five Solas series)
    Includes bibliographical references.
    ISBN 978-0-310-51580-7 (softcover)
    1. Glory of God—Christianity. 2. Reformed Church—Doctrines. I. Title.
BT180.G6V36 2015
231—dc23   201501936

Cover design: *Chris Tobias/Outerwear for Books*
Interior design: *Kait Lamphere*

Printed in the United States of America

HB 01.16.2024

Contents

A Note from the Series Editor

What doctrines could be more foundational to what it means to be an evangelical Protestant than the five *solas* (or *solae*) of the Reformation? In my experience, however, many in evangelical churches today have never heard of *sola Scriptura* (by Scripture alone), *sola gratia* (by grace alone), *sola fide* (by faith alone), *solus Christus* (by Christ alone), and *soli Deo gloria* (glory to God alone).

Now it could be that they have never heard the labels but would recognize the doctrines once told what each *sola* means. At least I pray so. But my suspicion is that for many churchgoers, even the content of these five *solas* is foreign, or worse, offensive. We live in a day when Scripture's authority is questioned, the exclusivity of Christ as mediator, as well as the necessity of saving faith, is offensive to pluralistic ears, and the glory of God in vocation is diminished by cultural accommodation. The temptation is to think that these five *solas* are museum pieces of a bygone era with little relevance for today's church. We disagree. We need these *solas* just as much today as the Reformers needed them in the sixteenth century.

The year 2017 will mark the five hundredth anniversary of the Reformation. These five volumes, each written by some of today's best theologians, celebrate that anniversary. Our aim is not merely to look to the past but to the present, demonstrating that we must drink deeply from the wells of the five *solas* in order to recover our theological bearings and find spiritual refreshment.

Post tenebras lux

Matthew Barrett, series editor

Acknowledgments

I would like to thank Matthew Barrett for asking me to join this Zondervan series on the Reformation *solas*. His unexpected invitation provided a good excuse to set aside some time from the research topics that ordinarily occupy my mind and to reflect on a topic—Glory to God Alone—that couldn't fail to be an edifying use of time.

I'm also very grateful to Christopher Chelpka, Zach Keele, and Shane Lems for their theological and pastoral insight in helping me to make this book better.

Thanks as always to Katherine for everything—even for reading a draft of the manuscript. Thanks to Jack for being such a happy housemate; what will I have to thank you for next time, when you'll be out of the house?

David VanDrunen

PART 1

The Glory of God in Reformed Theology

CHAPTER 1

Soli Deo Gloria Among the Reformation Solas

"It is not sufficient for anyone, and it does him no good
to recognize God in his glory and majesty, unless he
recognizes him in the humility and shame of the cross."
—*Martin Luther*

"We never truly glory in him until we have utterly discarded
our own glory. . . . The elect are justified by the Lord, in
order that they may glory in him, and in none else."
—*John Calvin*

Soli Deo Gloria—Glory to God alone. Most Protestant Christians do not read Latin these days, but many of them need no help translating these three words. What simple slogan stirs the godly heart more warmly and encapsulates more biblical truth than *soli Deo gloria*? "Glory to God" was the theme of the angelic host that announced Jesus' birth to the shepherds in the field and of the heavenly throng whose songs John recorded in Revelation. What a privilege almost beyond imagination that the all-majestic God calls sinners like us to contemplate his glory and to echo the angels' chorus in our own worship. And what a blessing that he enables us to write and read books on such a grand topic.

The occasion for this book, and the series of which it's a part, is to commemorate and celebrate the Protestant Reformation, whose unofficial 500th birthday draws near as I write. Protestants commonly speak of the "five *solas* of the Reformation," but we often forget that the Reformers themselves never sat down and adopted these five slogans—sola scriptura, sola fide, sola gratia, solus Christus, and *soli Deo gloria*—as the official mottos of the Reformation movement. At first, this sounds a little disappointing. We like to think we're adopting the very same set of phrases that Luther, Zwingli, Calvin, and their colleagues bequeathed to their spiritual posterity.

It really shouldn't disappoint us at all. People may have begun speaking of the "five *solas* of the Reformation" only long after the Reformation itself, but each of these five themes does in fact probe the heart of Reformation faith and life in its own way. The Reformers may not have spoken explicitly of "the five *solas*," but the magnification of Christ, grace, faith, Scripture, and God's glory—and these alone—suffused their theology and ethics, their worship and piety. Christ alone, and no other redeemer, is the mediator of our salvation. Grace alone, and not any human contribution, saves us. Faith alone, and no other human action, is the instrument by which we're saved. Scripture, and no merely human word, is our ultimate standard of authority. God's glory alone, and that of no creature, is the supreme end of all things. Our study of the five *solas* involves no rote repetition of slogans but the wonderful embrace of the holy religion taught in the Bible and revitalized in the Reformation.

Soli Deo Gloria: The Glue That Holds the *Solas* Together

Even so, there may seem to be something about *soli Deo gloria* that works less well than the other four as a motto summarizing Reformation theology. Teachers of Reformation theology, trying to be fair and accurate, often have to remind their students that medieval Christianity and sixteenth century Roman Catholicism did not deny the importance of Scripture, faith, grace, and Christ. Theologians spoke of them often and would have eagerly affirmed that there is no salvation without them. But if we could press the matter further and ask these theologians about the little word *alone*, we would soon find genuine disagreement. While the Reformers claimed that Scripture alone is the authority for Christian faith and life, Roman Catholics professed reverence for Scripture but insisted that the church's tradition and the Pope in Rome stood alongside Scripture to interpret it infallibly and to augment its teaching. When the Reformers asserted that justification comes by faith alone, Roman Catholics responded that justification does indeed come by faith, but also by works alongside faith. They had similar exchanges about grace and Christ.

Claims about Scripture alone, faith alone, grace alone, and Christ alone concerned the two chief points of debate between Rome and the Reformation: religious authority and the doctrine of salvation. *Soli Deo gloria* thus appears to be a bit of an outlier. When the Reformers proclaimed that glory belongs to God alone, did Roman Catholics really respond that glory in fact belongs equally to God and something or someone else? Does the principle of *soli Deo gloria*, magnificent as it is, really have much to do with the Reformation itself?

Indeed it does, even if Rome never directly denounced the idea of glory to God *alone* as it denounced the ideas of Scripture *alone* and faith *alone*. *Soli Deo gloria* can be understood as the glue that holds the other *solas* in place, or the center that draws the other *solas* into a grand, unified whole. Recent writers suggest the same idea when they speak of *soli Deo gloria* as "the logical implication of the other four points" or as the motto that "subsumes all the others."[1]

What justifies such strong claims? Simply put, the fact that salvation is by faith alone, grace alone, and Christ alone, without any meritorious contribution on our part, ensures that all glory is God's and not our own. Likewise, the fact that Scripture alone is our final authority, without any ecclesiastical tradition, magisterium, or Pope supplementing or overruling it, protects the glory of God against every human conceit. Rome, of course, would never admit to usurping God's glory. Even meritorious human works, it says, are accomplished by divine grace infused through the sacraments. The church's traditions grow organically from the practice of the apostles, Rome adds, and the Pope is the servant of servants. But the Reformers came to understand how such claims, though perennially attractive, ultimately reveal the deceit of the human heart. How we like to think that there's something for us to add to the satisfaction and obedience of Christ or to the inspired word of the prophets and apostles, and even that God is wonderfully honored by our contribution. But the Reformers perceived that the perfect word and work of Christ—precisely because they are perfect—need nothing to supplement them. Anything that tries to supplement them, in fact, challenges their perfection and thus dishonors God's word and work in Christ. If the Roman Catholic doctrine of authority and doctrine of salvation are true, all glory thus does not belong to God alone. And God, Scripture tells us, will share his glory with no other (Isa 42:8).

We might think of it in another way. By holding forth *soli Deo gloria* as the lifeblood of the *solas*, we remind ourselves that the biblical religion recaptured by the Reformation is not ultimately about ourselves, but about

1.   See respectively John D. Hannah, *How Do We Glorify God?* (Phillipsburg, NJ: P&R, 2000), 9; R. C. Sproul Jr., *"Soli Deo Gloria,"* in *After Darkness, Light: Distinctives of Reformed Theology: Essays in Honor of R. C. Sproul,* ed. R. C. Sproul Jr. (Phillipsburg, NJ: P&R, 2003), 191.

God. Our focus so easily becomes self-centered, even when we ask the same important questions that occupied the Reformers: Where can *I* find God's authoritative revelation? How can *I* escape the wrath of God? What must *I* do to be saved? The other four *solas* provide necessary and life-changing answers to such questions, but *soli Deo gloria* puts them in proper perspective: the highest purpose of God's plan of salvation in Christ, made known in Scripture, is not our own beatitude, wonderful as that is. The highest purpose is God's own glory. God glorifies himself through the abundant blessings he bestows upon us.

A Theology of Glory Vs. a Theology of the Cross: Martin Luther

As we embark on this study, some puzzling questions may arise for readers familiar with Reformation theology. Didn't Martin Luther speak *against* a "theology of glory"? Can an emphasis upon the glory of God actually detract from a biblical "theology of the cross" rather than illumine it? These are good questions. Luther did, in fact, call for a theology of the cross to replace the theology of glory he thought so prevalent in his own day, but his purpose was not to divert our attention from the glory of God. Rather, it was to explain *how* God manifests his glory to us and calls us to glorious fellowship with him. This is a great example of Luther's delight in paradox. Anyone who wishes to know the great God of glory must see him through the humility of the cross. Luther's reasoning is worth contemplating, because it exposes an important theme in subsequent chapters of this book: according to Scripture, glory comes through suffering. God is most highly glorified through the suffering of his Son; Christians know God and are glorified with Christ only by taking up their cross and following him.

Luther objected to the so-called theology of glory because he was concerned that Christians were seeking to know God in the wrong way. Many theologians thought they could understand the one true God by the speculative power of their own reason. They figured they could get to God directly and perceive him as he is in himself. Luther countered that we have no hope of knowing God unless he takes the initiative and reveals himself to us, and this strips us of our illusions of control. The theology of glory, therefore, is an exercise of human pretension. Sinful human beings, cloaking their hubris in a seemingly pious religiosity, try to climb to heaven to get a peek at God in his majesty. If we want to know God, Luther came to recognize, we must know him through revelation, and his clearest revelation is in Scripture. And when we open Scripture and learn that we are lost sinners, and that a God of wrath and judgment stands against us, the theology of glory becomes but a dream extinguished by Scripture's dawn.

In Scripture, however, Luther also discovered the theology of the cross. As long as sinful people strive to come to God by their own resources, the Almighty will keep himself veiled. But when they seek him through the humanly unimaginable way of the cross, God redeems them from sin and provides genuine knowledge of himself. To behold the God of glory, we must behold God beaten, mocked, and crucified. To gain everlasting beatitude, we must utterly humble ourselves and find refuge only in a cursed cross.

It may be helpful to hear this in a few of Luther's own words. Some of his most famous statements about the theology of glory and theology of the cross come from the *Heidelberg Disputation*, composed in 1518, during his early efforts at reformation. Luther identifies two kinds of theologians. One is the "theologian of the cross": he "who comprehends the visible and manifest things of God seen through suffering and the cross" is the one who deserves to be called a theologian. "It is not sufficient for anyone," writes Luther, "and it does him no good to recognize God in his glory and majesty, unless he recognizes him in the humility and shame of the cross." On the other hand, Luther describes the "theologian of glory" in this way: he "who does not know Christ does not know God hidden in suffering. Therefore he prefers works to suffering, glory to the cross, strength to weakness, wisdom to folly, and, in general, good to evil." The "theologian of the cross," in contrast, has been "deflated and destroyed by suffering and evil until he knows that he is worthless and that his works are not his but God's."[2]

As it turns out, Luther's critique of the theology of glory was hardly opposed to the perspective summarized at the opening of this chapter. I noted that the two overriding concerns of the Reformation had to do with religious authority and the doctrine of salvation. Luther championed the theology of the cross as a result of the same concerns. The theology of the cross was built upon biblical revelation that rejected all speculative human attempts to know God in our own way.[3] The theology of the cross was also

---

2. *Luther's Works*, vol. 31, *Career of the Reformer: I*, ed. Harold J. Grimm, gen. ed. Helmut T. Lehmann (Philadelphia: Fortress, 1957), 52–53.

3. As Alister McGrath has put it, "We may summarize the leading features of the *theologia crucis* [theology of the cross] as follows: (1) The theology of the cross is a theology of revelation, which stands in sharp contrast to speculation." See *Luther's Theology of the Cross: Martin Luther's Theological Breakthrough* (Oxford: Basil Blackwell, 1985), 149.

a theology of salvation, rejecting all vain endeavors to reconcile ourselves to the creator.[4] It therefore points only to the grace of God in Christ, and summons us to confess our own poverty, to look outside of ourselves, and to cling only to Christ by faith. It hardly turns us away from God's glory altogether. God glorifies himself, and we can live for his glory, but only along a path that unaided human reason could never have discovered and would never have dared imagine. The way to God's glory winds through the lowliness and desolation of Calvary.

Divine Glory and Human Glory: John Calvin

The suspected tension between Luther's critique of the theology of glory and the Reformation theme of *soli Deo gloria* turns out to be no problem at all. A different sort of problem is perhaps more serious, since it threatens to challenge the whole thrust of Reformation theology we've considered thus far. The alleged problem is this: the emphasis on God's glory and God's glory *alone* seems to demean human beings. If God's glory implies humanity's debasement, is such a God really worthy of our praise? Furthermore, the problem continues, this depiction of human debasement is hardly consistent with Scripture. Scripture describes human beings as the pinnacle of God's creation, as divine image-bearers with dominion over the world. Even after the fall, God redeems his people so that someday they might be glorified. Surely if glorification awaits us, then glory does not belong to God *alone*!

This, too, is not really a problem, but it does present a challenge. I asked at the outset whether any simple slogan encapsulates as much truth as *soli Deo gloria*. I think the answer is probably no, yet by their very nature slogans simplify matters and fail to express nuance and complexity. If the *soli Deo gloria* theme is as profound as I've suggested, then we must attend to its nuance and complexity in order to do it justice. This alleged tension between the *soli Deo gloria* theme and the gift of human glorification is a great case in point.

Scripture does indeed speak of human experience and the human calling in many exalted ways. God made us in his image—just a little lower than the angels—and gave us dominion over the works of his hands (Gen 1:26–28; Ps. 8:5–8). Even more marvelous, God destined human beings

---

4.   Bernhard Lohse comments that "use of the concepts *theologia gloriae* and *theologia crucis* . . . helps to make the question of salvation the theme of his theology." See *Martin Luther's Theology: Its Historical and Systematic Development*, trans. Roy A. Harrisville (Minneapolis: Fortress, 1999), 38. For similar comments, see also McGrath, *Luther's Theology of the Cross*, 151, 174.

to rule the world to come (Heb 2:5–9). He has promised that those who believe in his Son, though guilty sinners, will share in Christ's glory and have glory revealed in them (Rom 8:17–18). At first blush, this does seem to contradict the Reformation slogan we so enthusiastically promote.

Yet we need not be embarrassed by the Bible's description of human exaltation. It is good that we feel the tension and wrestle with it, because we cannot fully understand the glory of God without giving due weight to humanity's glorification in creation and especially in redemption. One way to put it is that the all-wise and loving God is pleased to glorify himself precisely through the glorification of his human creation. Our glory, such as it is, redounds back to God's glory. From a different angle we might also say that precisely through acknowledging and seeking God's glory alone, human beings attain their highest destiny and enjoy their proper dignity. Our words are true and edifying when they conform to Scripture alone. Our works become good and holy when they proceed from justification by grace alone through faith alone. We are renewed in the image of God when we rest on Christ alone. So are human beings demeaned by the confession of glory to God alone? Unexpectedly, no. As the opening of both the Westminster Shorter and Larger Catechisms communicates, God simultaneously makes us instruments for glorifying him and causes us to enjoy him as we ascribe to him all glory: the "chief end of man" is "to glorify God, and to enjoy him forever." In God's glory is our dignity. In God's glory is our delight. Our glorification lies in ascribing all glory in heaven and earth to him.

The Reformers understood this. John Calvin provides a good example. In his zeal to protect the supreme glory of God, Calvin recognized that God manifests his glory in large part through the beauty of his handiwork. Calvin stood in awe of creation as a "beautiful theatre," indeed, a "theatre of the divine glory."[5] "In every part of the world," he writes, "some linea-ments of divine glory are beheld."[6] Appealing to biblical texts that describe God's revelation of his greatness through nature, Calvin observes: "Because the glory of his power and wisdom is more refulgent in the firmament, it is frequently designated as his palace. And, first, where you turn your eyes, there is no portion of the world, however minute, that does not exhibit at

---

5. Calvin, *Institutes of the Christian Religion*, trans. Henry Beveridge (Grand Rapids: Eerdmans, 1953) 1.14.20; and Calvin, *Calvin's Commentaries*, vol. 22 (Grand Rapids: Baker, 1999), 266 (concerning Hebrews 11:3). For helpful discussions of Calvin's view of the natural order and its revelation of God's glory, see e.g. Susan E. Schreiner, *The Theater of His Glory: Nature and the Natural Order in the Thought of John Calvin* (Durham: Labyrinth, 1991); and Davis A. Young, *John Calvin and the Natural World* (Lanham, MO: University Press of America, 2007).

6. *Institutes*, 1.15.3.

least some sparks of beauty; while it is impossible to contemplate the vast and beautiful fabric as it extends around, without being overwhelmed by the immense weight of glory."[7]

But Calvin also thought that God's glory shines in a special way in human beings, created in the image of God. Calvin located the image, and hence humanity's chief dignity, especially in the soul, yet he also comments: "There was no part even of the body in which some rays of glory did not shine," and thus "the divine glory is [also] displayed in man's outward appearance."[8] Calvin's zeal for the glory of God, therefore, hardly entailed a demeaning view of creation or of humanity in particular. In fact, it was just the opposite. The beauty and dignity we have, thought Calvin, reflect God's glory manifest in us.

If God's glory shines in the original creation, how much more does it radiate in Christ, his work of redemption, and the hope of new creation? "In the person of Christ," Calvin remarks, "the glory of God is visibly manifested to us."[9] The salvation achieved in Christ's incarnation also promotes the divine glory. When contemplating our justification in Christ, for example, Calvin asserts that "two ends must be kept especially in view—namely, that the glory of God be maintained unimpaired, and that our consciences, in the view of his tribunal, be secured in peaceful rest and calm tranquility."[10] We ought to remember, he adds, "that in the whole discussion concerning justification the great thing to be attended to is, that God's glory be maintained entire and unimpaired; since, as the Apostle declares, it was in demonstration of his own righteousness that he shed his favor upon us."

This statement is a wonderful example of how *soli Deo gloria* is so closely connected with the other Reformation *solas*. Salvation by Christ alone, through grace alone, by faith alone means that all glory goes to God alone. And far from demeaning us, this marvelous display of divine glory enables us to fulfill our highest calling. Even now, explains Calvin through his own "theology of the cross," we have the privilege of declaring God's glory as we cast aside our own: "We never truly glory in him until we have utterly discarded our own glory . . . The elect are justified by the Lord, in order that they may glory in him, and in none else."[11] But even this is nothing compared to the privilege that awaits the saints when Christ

---

7. Ibid., 1.5.1.
8. Ibid., 1.5.3.
9. Ibid., 3.2.1.
10. Ibid., 3.13.1.
11. Ibid., 3.13.2.

returns. Commenting on Titus 2:13, Calvin states: "I interpret the *glory of God* to mean not only that by which he shall be glorious in himself, but also that by which he shall then diffuse himself on all *sides*, so as to make all his elect partakers of it."[12]

The cynic's objection that the Reformation theme of *soli Deo gloria* debases humanity need not worry us. In fact, to find humanity debased, we need look no further than the imaginary universe of those who deny God's glory. If God is not the all-glorious creator and redeemer, then this world is random chaos, life is meaningless, and human destiny is the grave. The biblical and Reformation message of *soli Deo gloria*, on the other hand, directs our eyes to Christ's second coming, when God will reveal his glory most brilliantly and his people, saved by grace, will themselves be glorified with their Lord.[13] This, too, must be our theme in the chapters ahead.

The Glory of God in Contemporary Theology

Even the relatively brief survey in the pages above highlights the importance of the *soli Deo gloria* theme for the Reformation, a theme originating not with the Reformers but in Scripture itself. In light of its eminent pedigree, it's little wonder that many contemporary writers who embrace the Reformation continue to return to the theme of God's glory to unfold the message of Scripture and to describe the character of the Christian religion. They do so in many different ways, however. Most of their approaches are compatible, and I imagine most of them would appreciate the others' insights. In part, their different approaches stem from the richness of the *soli Deo gloria* motif in Scripture and the fact that this single jewel can be admired from various angles. While my own treatment of the subject in subsequent chapters comports with some of these approaches better than with others, my point in sampling them is not to critique any in particular but to provide readers with a sense of the contemporary landscape and to help us identify important aspects of the full biblical presentation of *soli Deo gloria*.

---

12. *Calvin's Commentaries*, 21: 320 (concerning Titus 2:13). For helpful discussion of God's glory in Christ and redemption through him, see Billy Kristanto, *Sola Dei Gloria: The Glory of God in the Thought of John Calvin* (New York: Peter Lang, 2011), Part 2.

13. Although I discuss only Luther and Calvin, other Protestants Reformers were also devoted to the glory of God as central for Christian faith and life. To give but one example, Heinrich Bullinger, a prominent Reformer in Zurich, wrote: "Whosoever is endued with the Spirit of God, whatsoever he shall either do or say will savour of the fear of God; finally, he shall say and do all things unto the glory of God: and all these things truly are freely and fully drawn out of the only fountain of the Holy Ghost." See Henry Bullinger, *The Decades of Henry Bullinger*, *The Fourth Decade*, ed. Thomas Harding (Cambridge: Cambridge University Press, 1851), 320.

One emphasis among some recent writers captures perhaps the most common way of thinking about the *soli Deo gloria* theme in popular imagination: *soli Deo gloria* is a call for believers to gear all of their pursuits for the glory of God. This emphasis seems to follow the spirit of the great musician and orthodox Lutheran Johann Sebastian Bach, who appended "SDG" to scores he composed.[14] Terry Johnson, for example, devotes two chapters to *soli Deo gloria* in a book on the Reformation *solas*, the first of which focuses upon the reform of worship and church government. Then he treats the theme in terms of being obedient to God in all areas of life and the impact it can have on our surrounding cultures. He urges that *soli Deo gloria* calls believers today to "carry the Christian world-view into their realms of endeavor . . ."[15]

John Hannah raises similar ideas. He explains how "glory" expresses God's internal qualities or attributes and how Scripture often describes God's glory as a visible display of his brightness and excellency.[16] But central to Hannah's work—in accord with its title: *How Do We Glorify God?*—are the moral implications of God's glory. Our postmodern age, he observes, is one of radical self-centeredness and narcissism, but *soli Deo gloria* is "a call to a radical vision of God-centered living in all of life's many facets. The glory of God alone implies the right purpose for all of life—a God-centered purpose. All who share this radical view of Christianity make the ultimate purpose of life God's glory, not their own self-fulfillment or self-realization."[17] At some length, he later explains how God is glorified as we mirror his holiness and how this should transform our perspective on work, politics, and other endeavors of life.[18]

Reflecting on the theme of God's glory from a somewhat different angle, John Piper invokes the theology of Jonathan Edwards, and especially his treatise, "The End for Which God Created the World," about which I'll say a little more in the next chapter. Piper explains, "The *rejoicing* of all peoples in God, and the *magnifying* of God's glory are one end, not two. . . . The exhibition of God's glory and the deepest joy of human souls are one thing." This, he says, is what his own life is all about and

---

14. See Calvin R. Stapert, *My Only Comfort: Death, Deliverance, and Discipleship in the Music of Bach* (Grand Rapids: Eerdmans, 2000), 27–28; and Jaroslav Pelikan, *Bach Among the Theologians* (Philadelphia: Fortress, 1986), 140.

15. Terry L. Johnson, *The Case for Traditional Protestantism: The Solas of the Reformation* (Carlisle, PA: Banner of Truth, 2004), 162. The two chapters dealing with *soli Deo gloria* are 6–7.

16. John Hannah, *How Do We Glorify God? Basics of the Reformed Faith Series* (Phillipsburg, NJ: P&R, 2008), 6–7.

17. Ibid., 6–7, 9.

18. Ibid., 19–35, 38–40.

what shapes nearly everything he preaches and writes.[19] In this Edwardsian vision, God's grace enables us to grow into an ever-increasing delight in God, and "God is most glorified in us when we are most satisfied in him."[20] Thus, God zealously desires our joy just as much as he desires his own glory.[21] In this sense, Piper embraces C. S. Lewis's aphorism, *"It is a Christian duty, as you know, for everyone to be as happy as he can."*[22]

Another route by which contemporary writers approach the theme of God's glory is as an organizing theme of biblical theology. I use the term "biblical theology" here in a technical sense. Biblical theology—in distinction from other methods of doing theology, such as systematic theology and historical theology—explores the progress and organic development of theological themes and of the overall message of Scripture as the biblical canon moves from earlier books to later books. We can also think of this as movement within Scripture from less complete revelation of God to more complete, or as the gradual growth in the manifestation of God's truth from seed into full blossom. I raise this subject because several writers have recently identified the glory of God as the central theme of biblical theology, that is, the central theme of this unfolding, ever more profound revelation of God in Scripture.

One of them, James Hamilton, organizes his *Biblical Theology* around the motif of God's glory in his work of salvation and judgment through history. He acknowledges that God's glory "is like a many-faceted gem, which reflects and refracts light in ever-new, ever-unexpected ways as it is admired."[23] But Hamilton attempts to bring these various beams of divine glory together by suggesting that "the glory of God is the weight of the majestic goodness of who God is, and the resulting name, or reputation, that he gains from his revelation of himself as Creator, Sustainer, Judge, and Redeemer, perfect in justice and mercy, loving-kindness and truth."[24] Hamilton recognizes a movement in Scripture from the more limited and local manifestations of God's glory to Old Testament Israel toward the universal and eschatological goal of God's glory filling all the world.[25]

Thomas Schreiner also makes the glory of God a major strand of his

---

19. John Piper, *God's Passion for His Glory: Living the Vision of Jonathan Edwards* (Wheaton, IL: Crossway, 1998), 31–32.

20. Ibid., 34–35, 47.

21. Ibid., 34.

22. Ibid., 46 (italics his).

23. James M. Hamilton, *God's Glory in Salvation Through Judgment: A Biblical Theology* (Wheaton, IL: Crossway, 2010), 59.

24. Ibid., 56.

25. Ibid., 106, 116, 268–69, 343, 483.

Biblical Theology, as he did in earlier works on New Testament biblical theology and Paul.[26] Schreiner claims that Scripture uses the word "glory" "broadly to capture the supremacy of God in everything." He believes this has direct implication for our moral lives: "Human beings exist to obey, believe in, and praise God . . . God exercises an absolute claim upon the lives of all."[27] A third contemporary biblical theologian, G. K. Beale, also calls readers' attention to the centrality of God's glory at the outset of *A New Testament Biblical Theology*: "I contend that the goal of the New Testament storyline is God's glory, and that the main stepping-stone to that goal is Christ's establishment of an eschatological new-creational kingdom and its expansion." Beale's primary focus is upon this stepping-stone, the new creation, but only because many others have already argued effectively that the glory of God is Scripture's ultimate end.[28]

These contemporary authors testify to the continuing richness and vibrancy of the Reformation theme that glory belongs to God alone. Whether contemplating godly service in the world, Christian spirituality, or the developing revelation of God's salvation in Scripture, these writers find the glory of God a deep reservoir for theological reflection. That will be the case in subsequent chapters of this book as well.

All Glory Belongs to God and Not to Ourselves

In this book, we have set out to contemplate the glory of the Lord and the Reformation theme that all glory belongs to God. The Reformers established a trajectory that will surely not lead us astray. Against the perennial temptation to elevate our own words above God's and to pursue everlasting life by our own deeds, the Reformers called the church back to Scripture alone, to faith alone, to grace alone, and to Christ alone, and by so doing they reminded us that all glory belongs to God and not to ourselves. Approaching this God and knowing him truly requires us to humble ourselves and to seek him in the lowliness of the cross. Yet far from debasing us, humbling ourselves by faith in Christ crucified reconciles us to God and enables us to become the sort of creatures God made us to be. God grants us the privilege of reflecting his own glory as we grow in

---

26. Thomas R. Schreiner, *Paul: Apostle of God's Glory in Christ: A Pauline Theology* (Downers Grove, IL: InterVarsity Press, 2001); Thomas R. Schreiner, *New Testament Theology: Magnifying God in Christ* (Grand Rapids: Baker Academic, 2008); Thomas R. Schreiner, *The King in His Beauty: A Biblical Theology of the Old and New Testaments* (Grand Rapids: Baker Academic, 2013).

27. G. K. Beale, *A New Testament Biblical Theology: The Unfolding of the Old Testament in the New* (Grand Rapids: Baker Academic, 2011), 126.

28. Ibid., 16.

holiness and ascribe him glory in our worship, and by one day joining him in the glory of the new creation—which Scripture wonderfully calls our *glorification*. God draws supreme glory to himself, in part, by glorifying us. The Reformation theme of *soli Deo gloria* is indeed a beautiful aspect of the good news of the gospel.

Our chief interest in this book is to explore this theme further in Scripture and to consider how we might build on the Reformers' insights and gain a deeper and fuller picture of the glory of God and its implications for Christian faith and life. The contemporary writers discussed above encourage us to think this is still a noble and profitable task. But before moving directly to Scripture, we would do well to reflect also on how Reformed theologians between the time of the Reformation and the early twenty-first century presented this topic. In Chapter 2, therefore, we continue these initial historical reflections by turning to the age of Reformed Orthodoxy (so-called), where we find not a dry and stifling theology, as the name might suggest, but a rich and careful understanding of the glory of God, its revelation in history, and its wonderful benefits for Christ's saints.

The Glorious God, Glorified Through Us: *Soli Deo Gloria* in Reformed Theology

"What is the chief end of man? Man's chief end is to glorify God, and to enjoy him forever."
—*Westminster Shorter Catechism*

"It is the necessary consequence of his [God's] delighting in the glory of his nature that he delights in the emanation and effulgence of it." —*Jonathan Edwards*

"The 'glory of the Lord' is the splendor and brilliance that is inseparably associated with all of God's attributes and his self-revelation in nature and grace, the glorious form in which he everywhere appears to his creatures."
—*Herman Bavinck*

In popular conception, the Reformation motto *soli Deo gloria* is sometimes reduced to a call for moral action: we Christians should pursue all activities for the glory of God as our only supreme end. Of course, there is nothing untrue about this statement—a couple of biblical texts even make this point explicitly. But there seems to be something imbalanced about focusing the *soli Deo gloria* theme exclusively upon Christians acting for God's glory. For one thing, it produces the awkward and ironic result that *soli Deo gloria* becomes centered on *us*: how *we* are to act and what end *we* should pursue. These are important issues indeed, but when *soli Deo gloria* turns into a program for human cultural renewal, we may well suspect that what was meant to be a *theocentric* battle cry has been distorted by more than a little *anthropocentric* static.

Soli Deo Gloria Is All About Us? Correcting the Imbalance

Focusing *soli Deo gloria* solely on human conduct is also imbalanced in that it fails to reflect Scripture's careful presentation of the topic. On many occasions Scripture calls the saints to give glory to God in their worship, and in a couple of places it exhorts Christians to do all things for God's glory. But more often Scripture appeals to God's glory as a way of describing *God*, especially as he manifests himself through biblical history, climactically in the Lord Jesus Christ, his Holy Spirit, and the new creation where Christ now sits enthroned.

Soli Deo gloria has much to do with our Christian moral life, but biblical integrity demands that we first reckon with how the glory of God is truly about God himself. This is an excellent reason to turn to a perhaps unexpected topic: the glory of God in the theology of Reformed orthodoxy. "Reformed orthodoxy" refers to a period beginning in the mid-to later-sixteenth century and lasting until the early-to mid eighteenth century. During this period, many outstanding Reformed theologians sought to consolidate and build upon the insights of Martin Luther, John Calvin, and other eminent Protestant Reformers. They organized Reformed theology in coherent ways, worked out doctrines that the Reformers had not considered in detail, defended these doctrines against the attacks of non-Reformed theologians, and taught them effectively to subsequent generations of Reformed ministers.

When I describe it in this way, Reformed orthodoxy probably sounds like a noble cause to Reformed readers of this book. But many writers over the past century—including some Reformed writers—gave Reformed orthodoxy a bad name. These critics dismissed Reformed orthodox theology as dry and sterile, as rationalistic rather than biblical, as relying upon the logic of human reason more than upon the exegesis of God's word. Thankfully, a number of scholars have recently debunked these myths about Reformed orthodoxy and Reformed theologians are now beginning again to dig into these older theologians and rediscover a wealth of material long ignored.[1]

The glory of God provides an interesting illustration. Although I will not attempt anything resembling a thorough study of this topic among Reformed orthodox theologians, even the brief remarks I make should confirm that Reformed orthodoxy involves a rich and nuanced conception

---

1. E.g., see Richard A. Muller, *Post-Reformation Reformed Dogmatics: The Rise and Development of Reformed Orthodoxy, ca. 1520 to ca. 1725*, 4 vols. (Grand Rapids: Baker Academic, 2003); and *Protestant Scholasticism: Essays in Reassessment*, eds. Carl R. Trueman and R. Scott Clark (Carlisle: Paternoster, 1999).

of God's glory. These theologians recognized the biblical point I made above: the glory of God is first and foremost about God himself and how he reveals his glory in this world. Yet they also recognized secondarily that God glorifies his people and enables them to reflect his glory through their worship and holistic obedience. This balanced account should act as a helpful guide when we turn to the Bible in subsequent chapters and seek to understand the *soli Deo gloria* theme in a way that honors Scripture's own description of God's glory.

In this chapter, I first provide an overview of how Reformed orthodox theology understood the glory of God as summarized by a contemporary historian and illustrated by a seventeenth-century Reformed orthodox theologian. Then I describe how the Westminster Confession of Faith and Catechisms, great summaries of Reformed orthodox theology that have guided Presbyterian and other Reformed churches for centuries, weave the theme of God's glory into the fabric of Christian faith and life.

The Glory of God According to Edward Leigh

To lay out a few aspects of the Reformed orthodox understanding of God's glory, I rely on the work of Richard Muller, who has probably done more than anyone to revive appreciation for Reformed orthodoxy in recent decades. I also illustrate Muller's claims by referring to Reformed orthodox theologian Edward Leigh (1602–71), to whose work, *A Treatise of Divinity*, Muller frequently appeals. Leigh served in Parliament while it was waging the English civil war and overseeing the Westminster Assembly (about which see below). He was an Oxford-trained theologian well versed in classical, patristic, and Reformation writings and the author of several influential works.[2] We will see in Leigh's work an impressive appreciation for the breadth and richness of the glory of God and its revelation.

A first element of the Reformed orthodox conception is that God's glory describes an aspect of his nature. Muller writes: "God's glory is to be understood essentially, as one of the divine attributes but, moreover, as an attribute that eminently reflects and reveals the perfection of all the attributes."[3] Leigh begins his exposition of God's glory with this point. God's glory is "the infinite excellency of the Divine essence." Sometimes, he says, the glory of God in Scripture signifies "the very essence and nature

---

2.　See e.g. "Edward Leigh," in *Dictionary of National Biography*, vol. 32, ed. Sidney Lee (New York: Macmillan, 1892), 432–33.

3.　Muller, *Post-Reformation Reformed Dogmatics*, 3.547.

of God" and sometimes "some of God's Attributes." Leigh later explains that these describe the "internal" aspect of God's glory. As internal, the glory of God "is the excellency of his Divine nature," in that God "is infinitely worthy to be praised, admired and loved of all." God is glorious internally according to his "own knowledge, love, and delight in himself."[4]

Leigh also claims that God's glory is "external." As Muller puts it, "The divine glory may be considered as external, expressed both in the creation and 'in divine dispensations toward his church and his people.' In particular, this external glory refers to 'the manifestation of his perfections by their effects.'"[5] What does this mean? Leigh notes that God possesses internal glory from all eternity and he can never have any more of it than he's always had. But Scripture also speaks of God making "all things for himself or his glory." This is the external glory of God, which is expressed, for one thing, in "the Heavens and Earth, all these glorious creatures here below, which are said to show forth his glory," as declared in Psalm 19. These creatures are "the effects of his glorious wisdom and power." "As the glory of men consists in outward ornaments," Leigh explains, "so God's glory consists in having such creatures, men and Angels to be his followers." In addition, this external glory concerns "when men and Angels do know, love, and obey him, and praise him to all eternity."[6]

Thus, we can see that Leigh does not take long to speak about God's creatures glorifying him in all they do, though he is careful to ground this in the internal glory of God and to portray our knowing, loving, obeying, and praising God as God's own "ornament." Later, he explains further how it is that we can glorify God: "not by putting any excellency into him, but by taking notice of his excellency, and esteeming him accordingly, and making manifest this our high esteem of him."[7] Muller states, "This last category of the orthodox discussion of the divine glory yields a strong practical application . . . : from this doctrine we ought to learn, above all, to seek after God's glory, to 'labor to partake of God's image, that we might be partakers of his glory.'"[8] Theology was hardly a cold, intellectual exercise for these Reformed orthodox theologians. As we will see shortly in the Westminster Confession and Catechisms, they saw doctrine and life as interconnected, and the topic of God's glory illustrates this well.

---

4.   Edward Leigh, *A Treatise of Divinity* (London, 1662), 111–13.
5.   Muller, *Post-Reformation Reformed Dogmatics*, 3.550.
6.   Leigh, *A Treatise of Divinity*, 113.
7.   Ibid., 116.
8.   Muller, *Post-Reformation Reformed Dogmatics*, 550. Muller here quotes Leigh, *A Treatise of Divinity*, 117.

Leigh also notes that the Scriptures "every where extol the Majesty and glory of God."[9] In part, they do so by giving him grand titles such as the "God of glory," "King of glory," and "glorious father," as evident in Acts 7:2, Psalm 24:8, and Ephesians 1:17. Scripture also extols God's glory by affirming that "the whole earth is full of his glory" (Isa 6:3).

Leigh believed that God's glory is internal to his being and, in this sense, unknowable to any but himself. But God also manifests his glory in and to his creatures, and in this sense it is knowable to us as well. How exactly does God manifest his glory in the world? "Ordinarily," Leigh states, God's glory is manifest "in his word and works." "God made all things for his glory," and hence "all his works set forth his glory." His works include "those of creation and preservation or providence" and also those "upon the hearts of believers." In all of these, "God is glorious." But God also manifests his glory "extraordinarily," that is, "in the cloud, in apparitions and visions."[10] "The cloud" refers to the pillar of cloud and fire that led the Israelites through the wilderness toward the Promised Land. Muller points out, "As the exegetical foundations of the Reformed orthodox doctrine made clear, both the *maiestas* [majesty] and the *Gloria Dei* are most frequently taken as identifiers of the *Shechinah* [that is, the pillar of cloud and fire] and of the *kabod Adonai* [that is, "glory of the Lord"]."[11] In this, the Reformed orthodox theologians again show themselves to be careful students of Scripture. Scripture does indeed speak frequently of God's glory in terms of the cloud in the wilderness.

In the first chapter, we considered a potential objection to the Reformation's emphasis upon the glory of God alone: that this exaltation of God implies the debasement of humanity. We found that John Calvin spoke of God glorifying himself precisely through glorifying us, in part now in our sanctification and worship and most fully in the age to come. The Reformed orthodox theologians also appreciated this point. Toward the end of his treatise, Leigh notes the remarkable fact that God has "joined our happiness and his glory together," that is, God is glorified as our supreme joy is realized. Leigh goes on to say that "God will hereby give us glory" and he calls us often "to think of the personal glory and excellency which the Saints shall enjoy when they come to Heaven."[12] In what does this heavenly glory consist? Our bodies, Leigh says, will be perfect, incorruptible,

9. Leigh, *A Treatise of Divinity*, 113.
10. Ibid., 114.
11. Muller, *Post-Reformation Reformed Dogmatics*, 3.541.
12. Leigh, *A Treatise of Divinity*, 118, 120.

spiritual ("because they shall be upheld by the Spirit of God"), and glorious. Our souls will be freed from all spiritual evils, possibility of sin, and all apprehension of God's wrath. We will bear the image of God in a perfect way, "the will shall be fully satisfied with God, the conscience filled with peace, [and] the affections of love and joy shall have their full content."[13]

We've observed quite an amazing progression of thought in this Reformed orthodox theologian. Beginning with glory as an inner attribute of God's nature—fully knowable only to God himself—Leigh then describes God's external manifestation of his glory in all of his works: God not only makes his glory to shine in the heavens but also enables us to magnify him in our obedience and worship in this life. The story culminates with God bringing his people, perfected in body and soul, to enjoy the glory of the new creation with him. For Leigh and his Reformed orthodox colleagues, all glory belongs to God alone, but this is no abstract statement about a self-centered deity or a slogan motivating a moral program. *Soli Deo gloria* draws us into a biblical story of creation, providence, redemption, and consummation. God's desire to glorify himself sweeps us up to him in a plot whose unending finale lands us in the New Jerusalem where God is supremely glorified in our glorification.

The Glory of God According to Jonathan Edwards

Later Reformed theologians continued to think about God's glory along many of the same trajectories. Perhaps no theologian is more famous for his focus upon God's glory than the eighteenth-century American, Jonathan Edwards (1703–58). Edwards was a pastor and missionary in colonial Massachusetts and closely associated with the Great Awakening. A prolific writer, he remains today the most well-known theologian in American history. In recent years, John Piper has emphasized a key theme in Edwards' treatment of God's glory: God finds chief delight in his own glory, that is, in himself, but this is not something different from his delight in the happy state of his creatures, insofar as they reflect the image of his own nature and beauty. As Edwards puts it in his archaic but still understandable words: "It is the *necessary consequence* of his [God's] delighting in the glory of his nature that he delights in the emanation and effulgence of it."[14]

Many others have written about Edwards' theology, and I will not

---

13. Ibid., 120.
14. See Jonathan Edwards, "The End for Which God Created the World," in John Piper, *God's Passion for His Glory: Living the Vision of Jonathan Edwards* (Wheaton, IL: Crossway, 1998), 141, 163–64.

add to this literature. I simply observe here that Edwards' understanding of God's glory and its relation to us was not wholly original to him. Many years earlier, as we saw, Leigh claimed that God has "joined our happiness and his glory together." Edwards therefore unpacked a theme already long recognized among Reformed theologians. It is also helpful to remember that Edwards did not speak about God's glory solely in terms of his delight in our supreme God-centered happiness. He also had a keen sense of the broader biblical terrain that Leigh and other Reformed orthodox theologians had previously navigated. Edwards describes the Old Testament's use of the word "glory," for example, in terms reminiscent of Leigh's: "Sometimes it is used to signify what is *internal, inherent,* or in the *possession* of the person: and sometimes for *emanation, exhibition,* or *communication* of this internal glory; and sometimes for the *knowledge,* or *sense* of these, in those to whom the exhibition or communication is made; or an *expression* of this knowledge, sense, or effect." Edwards also notes that in Scripture, "the glory of God" sometimes signifies "the second person in the Trinity."[15] Despite his general thoroughness, Leigh had given little attention to this magnificent biblical theme.[16]

The Glory of God According to Herman Bavinck

I close this section with a few words from Herman Bavinck, a Dutch Reformed theologian of the late nineteenth and early twentieth centuries. Bavinck's *magnum opus, Reformed Dogmatics,* reflects the general spirit of Reformed orthodoxy perhaps better than any other piece of theological literature written since. When discussing God's glory, Bavinck draws together many of the themes we have observed in previous pages:

> The 'glory of the Lord' is the splendor and brilliance that is inseparably associated with all of God's attributes and his self-revelation in nature and grace, the glorious form in which he everywhere appears to his creatures. This glory and majesty . . . appeared to Israel . . . It filled the tabernacle and the temple . . . , and was communicated to all the people. . . . This glory is above all manifested in Christ, the

---

15. Ibid.," 230.

16. With respect to Christ, Leigh is most concerned to explain that God's infinite glory was *not* communicated to Jesus' human nature. This is a sound theological concern. Leigh did acknowledge that Christ's glory as mediator of salvation is "far above all creatures," though less than "a glory merely divine." See Leigh, *A Treatise of Divinity,* 116. Thus Leigh did not ignore Christ's glory, but I believe it is fair to conclude that he does not give sufficient attention to how God's glory is manifest in Christ, given the importance of this theme in Scripture, which we'll consider especially in Chapter 4.

only-begotten Son . . . and through him in the church . . . , which is looking for 'the blessed hope and the manifestation of the glory of our great God and Savior, Jesus Christ (Titus 2:13).[17]

The glory of God: an internal and eternal divine attribute, revealed in this world everywhere, yet especially to Israel of old and in these last days through his Son, in whose glorious second coming we find our own blessed hope. This trajectory of Reformed orthodox reflection provides an impressive paradigm to inspire and guide our own biblical study of *soli Deo gloria* in subsequent chapters.

The Glory of God According to the Westminster Confession of Faith and Catechisms

Thus far we have examined the Reformed orthodox theology of God's glory by considering a few individual theologians. Even this short exercise, I hope, has shown that Reformed orthodoxy, although thorough and precise, was hardly dry, boring, or impractical. Exploring this theme in the Westminster Confession and Catechisms may enable us to appreciate even more richly the biblical and spiritually edifying character of Reformed orthodox reflection on the glory of God.

Reformed theological reflection on Christian faith and life has never just been the task of individual theologians but also the task of the church as a body, a privilege in which all of its members share. Writing confessions and catechisms and putting them to use in the church's ministry is one important way in which Reformed Christians have carried out this privilege. These confessions and catechisms serve several mutually supportive purposes. They serve as a way to define publicly what the church believes, and hence, they become bonds of institutional unity by bringing many congregations together, committed to the same truths from God's Word. (For what it's worth, to "confess" literally has to do with speaking or acknowledging something *together*—confessing is something, by definition, one cannot do alone.) The Reformed confessions and catechisms serve, furthermore, as ways to define and test the theological soundness of leaders in the church, particularly its ministers. They have also functioned as wonderful teaching tools to instruct all the members of the body, whether youths, new converts, or long-time believers who stand in need of refreshment in the great truths of Scripture.

---

17. Herman Bavinck, *Reformed Dogmatics*, vol. 2, *God and Creation*, ed. John Bolt, trans. John Vriend (Grand Rapids: Baker Academic, 2004), 252.

Although the Reformed wrote many valuable confessions and catechisms in the decades following the Reformation, some of which are still beloved and utilized today, the composition of the Westminster Confession of Faith and the Westminster Shorter and Larger Catechisms was arguably their supreme effort. After these documents were written in the 1640s, the Reformed mostly ceased to write new confessions. Over one hundred theologians—mostly English pastors and professors—comprised the Westminster Assembly, the body that wrote these documents. While the Westminster Assembly was not a gathering of any one church (the English Parliament called and supervised the assembly), its legacy was thoroughly ecclesiastical. Subsequent historical events ensured that the assembly's work had no political import, but its confession and catechisms have been adopted by many Presbyterian and other Reformed churches around the world ever since. Numerous churches have united around their mutual confession of these "Westminster Standards." Thousands of preachers have been examined for the ministry in part through testing their knowledge and commitment to the doctrines they teach, and countless children have begun their theological instruction with the 107 questions and answers of the Shorter Catechism, which begins by asking, "What is the chief end of man?" and proceeds to answer, "Man's chief end is to glorify God, and to enjoy him forever."[18]

The Shorter (and Larger) Catechism begins, therefore, by pointing God's people to the glory of God, a theme which appears again and again in the confession and catechisms. These documents are the product of Reformed orthodoxy: a great many members of the Westminster Assembly were educated in and skilled practitioners of its theology. It's fascinating to see how Reformed orthodoxy perceived the centrality of the glory of God for Christian faith and life in these documents designed for the very practical purpose of uniting believers together and educating people, even the very young, in the essentials of Christianity. I will focus primarily on the confession, while also discussing the catechisms at various points along the way.

Examining the Westminster Confession of Faith (hereafter referred to as WCF) and the Larger and Shorter Catechisms (hereafter referred to as WLC and WSC, respectively) on the glory of God brings a twofold

---

18. For recent studies of the theology and context of these documents, see J. V. Fesko, *The Theology of the Westminster Standards: Historical Context & Theological Insights* (Wheaton, IL: Crossway, 2014); and Chad Van Dixhoorn, *Confessing the Faith: A Reader's Guide to the Westminster Confession of Faith* (Carlisle, PA: Banner of Truth, 2014).

truth to light: God is all-glorious and he glorifies himself in all his works. These documents' emphasis is not on *our own* conduct and how *we* bring glory to God through some sort of moral or cultural agenda. However, the WCF, WLC, and WSC do unpack God's self-glorification in a way that has much to do with us. An important way in which God glorifies himself, they teach, is by his gracious work of salvation, such that we Christians become God's own means for magnifying his glory: "God hath all life, glory, goodness, blessedness, in and of himself . . . , nor deriving any glory from them [his creatures], but only manifesting his own glory in, by, unto, and upon them."[19] This is a profound and deeply biblical truth to ponder. In and of ourselves, we cannot contribute a single speck to God's glory, but in God's self-glorification he manifests his glory unto us and upon us, such that he is glorified in us and by us. We can truly rejoice in *soli Deo Gloria* understood this way.

As with Reformed orthodox theology in general, the Westminster Confession and Catechisms view *glory* as an attribute of the one true God, that is, an essential aspect of his nature. The WLC begins its definition of God by stating, "God is a Spirit, in and of himself infinite in being, glory, blessedness, and perfection."[20] This true God is triune, and Father, Son, and Holy Spirit are "the same in substance, equal in power and glory."[21] This explains the statement above that ascribes to God "all life, glory, goodness, blessedness, in and of himself."[22] God needs no one and no thing to make him glorious. He himself is the origin and author of his glory.

The WCF proceeds to say that God also manifests his glory "in, by, unto, and upon them," that is, upon the creatures he's made.[23] In other words, God reveals externally, in the created world, the internal glory he has always possessed. Consider the many ways in which the WCF speaks of God glorifying himself through his works in the world. First, God glorifies himself through his revelation *in Scripture*. The "scope" of Scripture (that is, its focus or goal) is "to give all glory to God" and it sets forth "all things necessary for his own glory."[24] God also glorifies himself *in his plan for all of history*. God works "all things according to the counsel of his own immutable and most righteous will," and does so "for his own glory."[25]

---

19. *Westminster Confession of Faith*, 2.2.
20. *Westminster Larger Catechism*, 7.
21. Ibid., 9.
22. *Westminster Confession of Faith*, 2.2.
23. Ibid.
24. Ibid., 1.5 and 1.6.
25. Ibid., 2.1.

A crucial, though greatly mysterious, aspect of his counsel is his *decree of election and reprobation*: "By the decree of God, for the manifestation of his glory, some men and angels are predestinated unto everlasting life; and others foreordained to everlasting death."[26] This predestining unto life is "all to the praise of his glorious grace," while his dreadful passing by others redounds "to the praise of his glorious justice."[27] The theme of God's self-glorification continues as the WCF considers God's work in carrying out the eternal counsel of his will. God glorifies himself through his work of *creation*: "It pleased God the Father, Son, and Holy Ghost, for the manifestation of the glory of his eternal power, wisdom, and goodness, in the beginning, to create, or make of nothing, the world, and all things therein, whether visible or invisible, in the space of six days; and all very good."[28]

Having created the world, God also glorifies himself through his *providence*, that is, sustaining and ruling his handiwork: "God the great Creator of all things doth uphold, direct, dispose, and govern all creatures, actions, and things, from the greatest even to the least, by his most wise and holy providence . . . , to the praise of the glory of his wisdom, power, justice, goodness, and mercy."[29] This previous statement is truly all-encompassing. God superintends everything that happens in this world, and all of it transpires for the praise of his glory. The WCF insists that this includes tragic and evil events, though God is in no way the author of sin.[30] God even governed *the fall of the human race*, that fount of all the world's evil: "This their [Adam's and Eve's] sin, God was pleased, according to his wise and holy counsel, to permit, having purposed to order it to his own glory."[31] He also manifests his glory in the providential establishment of government officials: "God, the supreme Lord and King of all the world, hath ordained civil magistrates, to be, under him, over the people, for his own glory, and the public good."[32]

His work of redemption, however, is the most amazing way in which God manifests his glory in, by, unto, and upon creation. He glorifies himself by calling us, sinful as we are, to participate in his own glory. The WCF speaks of this in all sorts of wonderful ways. For one thing, God's eternal election of his people manifests *his* glory by choosing *us* "unto everlasting

---

26. Ibid., 2.3.
27. Ibid., 2.5 and 2.7.
28. Ibid., 4.1.
29. Ibid., 5.1.
30. Ibid., 5.4.
31. Ibid., 5.4 and 6.1.
32. Ibid., 23.1.

glory."[33] The WCF also calls our future life in the heavenly kingdom "the state of glory," in which God will finally make us "perfectly and immutably free to good alone."[34] Later, it refers to our "eternal life at the hand of God" as "the glory to come."[35] Those who believe in God, love him, and strive to walk in good conscience before him, the WCF adds later, not only may be assured of their salvation here and now but may also "rejoice in the hope of the glory of God, which hope shall never make them ashamed."[36] We his saints, united to Christ by his Spirit and by faith, "have fellowship with him in his graces, sufferings, death, resurrection, and glory."[37]

The WLC elaborates upon this theme by speaking of believers' fellowship with Christ in glory as unfolding in three stages: in this life we enjoy "the firstfruits of glory with Christ," at death we will "behold the face of God in light and glory," and following the resurrection and final judgment we will enjoy "perfect and full communion . . . with Christ in glory."[38] The WCF concludes with multiple references to God's glorification through our glorification in the age to come. God has appointed the final judgment in part for "the manifestation of the glory of his mercy," and though he will raise up the wicked unto "dishonor," he will raise the bodies of his people, "by his Spirit, unto honor," and will make them "conformable to his [Christ's] own glorious body."[39]

In all of these ways, God manifests his glory through the saving of his people. Do the Westminster Standards, as part of this broader theme, also speak of God enabling us to glorify him through our own conduct? This is not a major concern of the WCF. In fact, it mentions this only once, when describing the good works believers do in obedience to God's commandments as evidence of their faith. These good works serve a number of beneficial functions: "by them believers manifest their thankfulness, strengthen their assurance, edify their brethren, adorn the profession of the gospel, stop the mouths of the adversaries, and glorify God."[40] The only other time the WCF raises the issue of people acting for God's glory, later in the same chapter, it explains that unbelievers, in part because they never act for "a right end, the glory of God," are unable to do good

---

33. Ibid., 2.3, 2.5, 2.6.
34. Ibid., 9.5.
35. Ibid., 16.5.
36. Ibid., 18.1.
37. Ibid., 26.1.
38. *Westminster Larger Catechism*, 82, 83, 86, 90.
39. *Westminster Confession of Faith*, 33.2 and 32.3.
40. Ibid., 16.2.

works.[41] Although pursuing God's glory is a minor theme in the WCF, the WCF does communicate this important point: only believers in Jesus Christ can act for God's glory, and for this reason, only they can do works truly pleasing to God.

The WCF gives minimal attention to our responsibility to glorify God, but the theme arises many times in the catechisms. The first question and answer of both catechisms announces that our chief end—that is, the primary goal and purpose of our entire existence—is to glorify God and enjoy him forever. This is a grand statement, but what does it mean? How do the catechisms envision us living to glorify God? Chapter 16 of the WCF, we saw above, indicates that *all* of our works should be done for God's glory, so the catechisms surely don't teach that we should glorify God only in a narrow slice of life. But it is striking that with only one exception, the catechisms speak of our giving glory to God in the context of *worship*.[42] It seems no stretch to say that they exhort us to glorify God most especially in laying aside our ordinary responsibilities and calling upon the Lord.

One place this emphasis emerges is precisely where we'd expect: the exposition of the first of the Ten Commandments, which calls us to have no other gods but the Lord. WSC 46 asks "What is required in the first commandment?" and answers, "to know and acknowledge God to be the only true God, and our God; and to worship and glorify him accordingly." WLC unpacks this focus on worship, explaining that we should worship and glorify God "by thinking, meditating, remembering, highly esteeming, honoring, adoring, choosing, loving, desiring, [and] fearing of him," as well as by "calling upon him, [and] giving all praise and thanks . . . to him with the whole man."[43] While not every action WLC 104 commends is an act of worship per se, it seems clear that the document envisions the whole-hearted devotion toward God required in the first commandment as centered on our public and private worship.

The catechisms also call us to glorify God in our worship through their instruction on prayer, for which the Lord's Prayer is a model. In the first petition of the Lord's Prayer, we call out, "Hallowed be thy name." According to the WSC, with these words we pray that "God would enable us, and others, to glorify him in all that whereby he maketh himself known; and that he would dispose all things to his own glory."[44] WLC

---

41. Ibid., 16.7.
42. The one exception is WLC 129, which calls on people in positions of authority to "procure glory to God" by faithfully executing their duties toward those under them.
43. *Westminster Larger Catechism*, 104.
44. *Westminster Shorter Catechism*, 101.

190 expands on these points. According to the catechisms, at the very outset of prayer, we rightly ask God to glorify himself and to empower us to glorify him.

This focus continues in subsequent petitions. WLC 184 asks what things we should pray for, and then states, "We are to pray for all things tending to the glory of God." There's a similar tenor inherent in the third commandment. Not taking the Lord's name in vain requires "that the name of God . . . be holily and reverently used . . . to the glory of God."[45] While God's name may be used properly outside of worship, worship is what WLC 112 highlights. We should holily and reverently use not only his name, but also his "ordinances, the word, sacraments, prayer, oaths, [and] vows."

Finally, focusing on the public, corporate worship of God, WLC 159 asks how the word of God is "to be preached by those that are called thereunto." The section concludes by calling upon ministers to preach "with fervent love to God and the souls of his people; sincerely, aiming at his glory, and their conversion, edification, and salvation."

This survey suggests that the Westminster Standards provide a fitting summary of Reformed orthodox teaching on the glory of God. Glory is an attribute of God's eternal being, derived only and solely from himself. Yet God is pleased to manifest his glory in and through the world he created. He glorifies himself in Scripture, in his works of creation and providence, and most amazingly by redeeming his people, who glorify him in all of their obedience and especially in worship, and whom he will bring one day to heavenly glory to attain that chief end for which he made the human race in the first place, to glorify and enjoy him forever. *Soli Deo gloria* would not be a bad way to summarize the Westminster Confession and Catechisms.

First Things First: God Glorifies Himself

I opened this chapter by warning against the ironic popular tendency to speak of *soli Deo gloria* as if this Reformation motto were primarily about ourselves and the way we act and shape our moral and cultural agendas. While God's glory should indeed be Christians' chief motive and goal in all our conduct, we must remember above all that glory *is* the Lord's and that in all his works *he* glorifies *himself.* With this truth at the center, we are able to recognize our call to glorify God for what it really is: God's work *in*

---

45. *Westminster Larger Catechism,* 112.

us so that he manifests his glory *through* us. How astounding that the way God seems most delighted to glorify himself is by enabling his treasured people to enjoy him in the glory of the new creation.

Reformed orthodoxy, especially through the Westminster Confession and Catechisms, helps us maintain our theological balance when contemplating *soli Deo gloria*. This great Reformation motto is about God from first to last, yet by his grace it has everything to do with his work in us and through us. Fortified with this hearty fare from the Reformed theological heritage, we now turn to Scripture to observe for ourselves how God manifests his glory in the unfolding of biblical history.

PART 2

The Glory of God in Scripture

CHAPTER 3

In the Cloud: God's Glory Made Visible

"Help us, God our Savior, for the glory of your name;
deliver us and forgive our sins for your name's sake."
—Psalm 79:9

"Not to us, LORD, not to us but to your name be the glory."
—Psalm 115:1

"I will not yield my glory to another."
—Isaiah 48:11

In the opening two chapters we considered how a common emphasis in contemporary discussion of *soli Deo gloria*—that we are to glorify God in all of our pursuits—gets at one important aspect of the Reformation theology of the glory of God but risks distorting its larger message. *Soli Deo gloria* was never primarily about us and our conduct but about God. According to Reformed orthodox theology, God is inherently glorious and he glorifies himself in all of his works. That is the heart of the matter. But how God glorifies himself in all of his works is striking and awe-inspiring. The eternally all-glorious God reveals his glory in and through this world, which evokes our praise and service, which redounds to God's glory. What's more, God glorifies himself in part by glorifying *us*, such that we, in Christ and by the Spirit, attain everlasting blessedness precisely through God's supreme self-glorification. God's great plan in history is to display his glory, and we get swept up in that plan. God delights to glorify himself through calling and enabling lost sinners to glorify and enjoy him forever. What a privilege. And how wonderfully consistent with other great *solas* of the Reformation: *sola fide, sola gratia*, and *solus Christus*.

The other Reformation *sola, sola scriptura*, drives us behind

43

Reformation theology to explore its source. The Reformation vision of God's glory is compelling and inspiring, but we need to know whether it grows out of biblical teaching. Here in Part 2, we turn to Scripture and find great reason to admire the biblical insight of Reformation and Reformed orthodox theologians. Their vision of God's glory captures Scripture's teaching beautifully.

But how best to approach this subject in Scripture? Obviously, there is no single way to unpack a theme so rich and intricate, but I propose to do so primarily by means of a story. Scripture itself is a grand story that moves from God's creation of the world to its fall, followed by a long history of redemption whose culmination begins in the incarnation, crucifixion, and exaltation of the promised Messiah and ends in his triumphant return and revelation of the new creation. Rather than examine God's glory in Scripture through the study of discrete sub-topics, I invite you to explore with me how the theme of God's glory tracks and beautifies this biblical story. In fact, the larger story of Scripture is in many respects the story of the revelation of God's glory.

We'll explore this theme in the next three chapters. This chapter begins the investigation where Scripture itself first points readers explicitly to God's glory: in the pillar of cloud and fire, which led the Israelites through the wilderness toward the Promised Land, inhabited its tabernacle and later its temple, and tragically abandoned its people in judgment for their great sins. In Chapters 4 and 5, I continue this story, whose success seems to hang in such precarious balance through much of the Old Testament. These chapters will trace how God brings his promises to fruition despite the rebellion of his people. He does so through a Savior whose glory is veiled for a time in abject humility but unveiled forevermore as king of his heavenly temple, attended by a once sinful people glorified in him.

The Glory of God: Prologue

Everyone loves stories, but sometimes a storyteller needs to provide some background in order for the audience to understand his tale. That may be true here. We want to proceed promptly to the biblical story of God's glory, but a few aspects of Scripture's presentation of divine glory do not fit into one particular place in the story although they provide very helpful background for it. In this opening section of the chapter, I want to unpack four of them as a kind of prologue to the story about to unfold.

First, both the Old and New Testaments use "glory" as a name for God.

He is the "Glory of Israel" (1 Sam 15:29), the "King of glory" (Ps 24:8, 9, 10), and the "God of glory" (Ps 29:3). When Stephen recounts the great deeds of God before the Sanhedrin, he begins by borrowing this latter Old Testament divine title: "Brothers and fathers, listen to me! The God of glory appeared to our father Abraham . . ." (Acts 7:2). Though rare in the Old Testament, the New Testament often calls God "Father," and Paul combines this new covenant title with the ancient theme of God's glory: the "God of our Lord Jesus Christ" is "the glorious Father," or, more literally, the "Father of glory" (Eph 1:17). In the Old Testament the special covenant name for God was the so-called "tetragrammaton," which orthodox Jews today do not pronounce and which Christians commonly translate "Yahweh" or "LORD." This name, said Moses to the Israelites, is "glorious and awesome" (Deut 28:58).

In Scripture, God's names are not arbitrary or random, but tell us something about who God is. By calling him the "Almighty," the "Most High," or the "Holy One," for example, Scripture provides a glimpse into his character. Thus, when Scripture calls him the God, King, or Father of glory, it indicates that God's very nature is glorious. This confirms the Reformed orthodox claim that glory is, first and foremost, internal to God: it is one of the divine attributes. We gladly affirm this, yet recognize the limits of our comprehension. God alone knows what exactly constitutes his internal glory; our finite minds cannot penetrate it. But we know that as God manifests his glory in the world, we see a reflection of that internal glory, the glory the Son enjoyed with the Father before all ages (cf. John 17:5).

Second, Scripture speaks of God's glory in terms of his honor or reputation or him being worthy of praise. We often associate having a "good name" with having a good reputation, and so it is with God. The God whose name is Glory deserves all praise and honor. As the Psalmist puts it, "Not to us, LORD, not to us but to your name be the glory" (Ps 115:1). In the second part of Isaiah this idea emerges with particular force. God says, for example, "I am the LORD; that is my name! I will not yield my glory to another or my praise to idols" (Isa 42:8); and later: "For my own sake, for my own sake, I do this. How can I let myself be defamed? I will not yield my glory to another" (Isa 48:11). Such texts illustrate the close biblical connection between God doing things for his own glory, for his own name, and for his own sake—each of these pertains to God's reputation as the one worthy of all honor. Likewise, the Psalms declare:

Help us, God our Savior, for the glory of your name; deliver us and forgive our sins for your name's sake (Ps 79:9).

The nations will fear the name of the LORD, all the kings of the earth will revere your glory (Ps 102:15).

As Jonathan Edwards claimed: "God's *name* and his *glory*, at least very often, signify the same thing in Scripture."[1]

Third, God reveals his glory in the created order. Under the first point I observed that God is internally glorious, but that we can really only perceive his glory as he manifests it in the world. One way he does this is through the beauty of creation. Most famously, Psalm 19 begins, "The heavens declare the glory of God; the skies proclaim the work of his hands." It's probably best to understand this in light of Paul's statement: "What may be known about God is plain to them [human beings], because God has made it plain to them. For since the creation of the world God's invisible qualities—his eternal power and divine nature—have been clearly seen, being understood from what has been made" (Rom 1:19–20). The theological term for this is *natural revelation*. God reveals himself in "what has been made," that is, in nature itself. Psalm 19 indicates, therefore, that glory is among God's "invisible qualities," which nature reveals. A number of other Psalms also associate God's glory with the heavens above. Several verses, for example, call out: "Be exalted, O God, above the heavens; let your glory be over all the earth" (Pss 57:5, 11; 108:5). Psalm 113:4 adds, "The LORD is exalted over all the nations, his glory above the heavens."

Finally, God has glorified himself through his great deeds in this world. In a sense, the preceding point was just a sub-point of this one: among God's great deeds are the making and sustaining of the created order in all its beauty. But while the third point above focuses on God's *natural* revelation, this fourth point looks to God's *special* revelation, such as the miraculous deeds by which he judges his enemies and redeems his people. These, too, make his glory known.

God glorifies himself through judging his enemies. Before the Israelites marched through the sea, God declared that he would "gain glory . . . through Pharaoh" by destroying his chariots and horsemen (Exod 14:4, 17–18). Later, God tells Sidon that in their midst he would "display [his] glory" (Ezek 28:22) and foretells a "memorable day" in which he will again "display [his] glory" through the destruction of Gog (Ezek 39:13).

---

1. See Jonathan Edwards, "Concerning the End for Which God Created the World," in *Works of Jonathan Edwards.* Vol. 8, *Ethical Writings,* ed. Paul Ramsey (New Haven: Yale University Press: 1989), 523. Also see John Piper, *God's Passion for His Glory,* 239.

Scripture emphasizes how God glorifies himself through the salvation of his people (which he accomplishes, in part, by destroying their enemies). For his glory God formed a people of his own, who are called by his name (Isa 43:7), and he is glorified in their prosperity: "You have enlarged the nation, LORD; you have enlarged the nation. You have gained glory for yourself; you have extended all the borders of the land" (Isa 26:15). Paul explains that in God's great plan of salvation—established from eternity (Eph 1:11)—we who have believed the gospel and been marked by the Spirit are his own possession, and this all (he says twice) is to "the praise of his glory" (Eph 1:12–14). Paul turns a similar phrase in Philippians to describe the effect of God's sanctifying work in our hearts: it is all "to the glory and praise of God" (Phil 1:9–11). As Jesus said, "This is to my Father's glory, that you bear much fruit, showing yourselves to be my disciples" (John 15:8).

In Chapter 5 we will consider in significantly more detail how God glorifies himself in the salvation of his people. But it is worth mentioning here that God brings glory to himself through saving his people by his *sovereign* power. Ephesians 1 makes this especially clear. Here Paul discusses many aspects of our salvation, including our sanctification (verse 4), adoption as sons (verse 5), forgiveness of sins (verse 7), and receipt of the Holy Spirit (verse 13). God planned and carried this out in his unique sovereignty. It all transpires "in accordance with his pleasure and will" (verse 5), "the mystery of his will" (verse 9), and "the purpose of his will" (verse 11). In the next chapter Paul famously adds: "For by grace you have been saved through faith—and this is not from yourselves, it is the gift of God—not by works, so that no one can boast" (Eph 2:8–9). Another way to describe this is that salvation is *monergistic*, that is, the work of God alone. This sovereign execution of salvation, furthermore, redounds to "the praise of his glorious grace" (Eph 1:6) and the "praise of his glory" (Eph 1:14). The historic Reformation conviction that *soli Deo gloria* is essentially connected to salvation from Christ alone, by grace alone, through faith alone is biblically well founded.

God thus glorifies himself in his created order generally and in his special acts of judgment and salvation in the world. I have offered just a tiny sampling of how this latter theme plays out through the Scriptures, but it provides a good transition to the main theme of this chapter, and indeed the theme of Chapters 3–5 as a whole. How is it that God glorifies himself through his special deeds in history? What is his master plan and how does it unfold?

God's Glory Revealed in a Cloud

In recent years, first-world economies have become increasingly dependent upon "the cloud." The cloud, in this context, has nothing to do with the sky or the weather, but with computing and data storage. In the quest for ever greater efficiency, we have been disposing of physical disks and drives of various sorts and housing more and more information in the cloud. Though the cloud has drawbacks—security, for example—its lure is obvious. One of its great attractions is that it does not take up space, at least not our own space. It helps us clear out the accumulated material and endless files that clutter our offices and closets.

It is interesting that we use the term "cloud" in this context to describe something invisible. The ordinary clouds in the sky are not veiled from sight. We look at them and anticipate a storm, we admire their beauty at sunset, and we know our airplane is reaching cruising altitude when we see them below us rather than above us. Sometimes we see an odd-shaped cloud and stop what we're doing simply to look and wonder for a few moments. Real clouds are physical, visible things.

This observation is strikingly relevant for our study of God's glory, and that's because Scripture so often describes the glory of God as revealed visibly *in a cloud*: the pillar of cloud that led the Israelites through the wilderness from Mount Sinai to the Promised Land. Readers may be surprised to learn that the book of Genesis never once refers to God as glorious. Granted, it often describes God in ways that seem glorious, but it does not use the term "glory" to describe the One who creates the world, later destroys it with a flood, chooses Abraham, Isaac, and Jacob, and does many other magnificent things. But the book of Exodus brings the glory of God to explicit prominence, and here and throughout the rest of the Pentateuch (that is, the first five books of Scripture), the language expressing God's glory is focused especially on the awesome cloud that protects and leads the Israelites on her desert pilgrimage. God is internally glorious, but he manifests his glory *visibly* in this world.

Since Exodus is where Scripture begins speaking explicitly about the glory of God, it seems fitting that we also begin at this point. What we will see over the next few chapters is that though the Israelites needed the cloud only during their wilderness trek, this revelation of God's glory was only the beginning of a long and beautiful story that weaves its way throughout the rest of Scripture and concludes with the glory of the age to come. The pillar of cloud and fire in certain respects initiates the story of God drawing near to his sinful people, of God sending his Son in deep humility and exalting him in supreme majesty, of God pouring out his Holy Spirit, and of God glorifying us with Christ for blessed life in the new creation. What first appeared to the Israelites in the barren wasteland ultimately becomes the everlasting dwelling of God with his people.[2] The story of God's glory is inseparable from his plan for history and the salvation of sinners.

What did the cloud actually look like? Scripture indicates that it was an awesome sight, but provides relatively few details. It must have been massive and bright, in order to be visible to all the people and even to provide them with light to see by night (cf. Exod 13:21). It was also mobile. Ordinarily it went in front of the people to show their path of travel, but it would also halt for periods of time, resting on Mount Sinai, for example, or instructing the Israelites to rest and camp at various places in the wilderness (e.g., Exod 13:21–22; 19:9; 40:36–37; Num 9:17–23). Once it even moved to the rear, to serve as a wall between the Israelites and the Egyptian army that pursued them toward the sea (Exod 14:19–20). We cannot say for sure what its features were, but Scripture describes it more like an imposing storm cloud than a white puffy cloud floating through the sky on a beautiful day. It covered Mount Sinai as a "dense cloud" (Exod 19:9), "like smoke from a furnace" (Exod 19:18), and produced thunder and lightning (Exod 19:16). The cloud's appearance at Sinai, however, seems to have been unusually intimidating, so presumably it could also appear in milder forms. The one other thing we know about the cloud's appearance is that during the night it "looked like fire" (Num 9:15–16; cf. Exod 40:38). This served, at least in part, to illumine the Israelites' path for nighttime travel (Exod 13:21). Putting these various clues together, I surmise that "the cloud" was like a brilliant fire surrounded by dense smoke; daylight dimmed the appearance of the fire while its brightness shone in the dark.[3]

As magnificent as the cloud's outward appearance must have been, its most awesome feature was that it was God's dwelling place. Scripture portrays God as sitting enthroned among his angelic host in the midst of this cloud. Psalm 97 begins, "The LORD reigns, let the earth be glad; let the distant shores rejoice. Clouds and thick darkness surround him; righteousness and justice are the foundation of his throne" (Ps 97:1–2). The imagery here is of clouds and thick darkness surrounding God as

---

2. For a good short summary of this cloud's story through biblical history, see Meredith G. Kline, *Images of the Spirit* (Grand Rapids: Baker, 1980), 17.

3. On the cloud and its appearance, also see Jacob Milgrom, *The JPS Torah Commentary: Numbers* (Philadelphia: Jewish Publication Society, 1990), 70–71; and Cornelis Houtman, *Exodus*, vol. 2 (Kampen, the Netherlands: Kok, 1996), 254.

he rules from his throne in justice. Psalm 99 contributes to this picture: "The LORD reigns, let the nations tremble; he sits enthroned between the cherubim" (Ps 99:1). Immediately thereafter it calls the Lord great "in Zion" (Ps 99:2), so we may suspect it refers simply to the tabernacle and later the temple in Jerusalem, where the two cherubim hovered over the ark of the covenant. But the psalmist has more in mind than just the temple, for he writes later: "He spoke to them [Moses and Aaron] from the pillar of cloud; they kept his statutes and the decrees he gave them" (Ps 99:7). Psalm 99 thus seems to view the earthly tabernacle, with its ark and cherubim, as a replica of a sanctuary in the cloud, where real-life angels hovered over the throne of the living God. When Scripture comments that "the glory of the LORD" appeared in the cloud (e.g., Exod 16:10), the reason is striking: it is because the Lord himself sat in its midst. Of course, even the cloud did not house *the* throne of God. The cloud itself was a replica, a brilliant image of God's heavenly temple that is altogether invisible to our eyes (for now!).

One other feature of the cloud is worth identifying before we trace its movement in the wilderness: Scripture associates the cloud especially with the Holy Spirit. In Deuteronomy the Song of Moses points us in this direction: "In a desert land he found him, in a barren and howling waste. He shielded him and cared for him; he guarded him as the apple of his eye, like an eagle that stirs up its nest and hovers over its young, that spreads its wings to catch them and carries them aloft" (Deut 32:10–11). These verses use some unusual Hebrew words that direct us back to their first use in Scripture: "Now the earth was formless and empty, darkness was over the surface of the deep, and the Spirit of God was hovering over the waters" (Gen 1:2). The cloud hovered over the Israelites in the barren waste just as the Spirit hovered over the barren waste of the original creation.

Perhaps this is like a coincidence, or a loose analogy. But later in Israel's history, the Old Testament confirms this association of cloud and Spirit and even seems to identify them. For example, Isaiah states:

> Then his people recalled the days of old, the days of Moses and his people—where is he who brought them through the sea, with the shepherd of his flock? Where is he who set his Holy Spirit among them, who sent his glorious arm of power to be at Moses' right hand, who divided the waters before them, to gain for himself everlasting renown, who led them through the depths? . . . They were given rest by the Spirit of the LORD. This is how you guided your people to make for yourself a glorious name (Isa 63:11–14).

Likewise, in the days of Ezra, the Israelites prayed: "Because of your great compassion you did not abandon them in the wilderness. By day the pillar of cloud did not fail to guide them on their path, nor the pillar of fire by night to shine on the way they were to take. You gave your good Spirit to instruct them" (Neh 9:19–20; cf. Hag 2:5). Although the one God clearly reveals himself as three persons only in the New Testament, the Old Testament describes this same truth in many preliminary ways. The cloud is the visible manifestation of the Spirit, and the throne of God sits within.[4]

This initial description of the glory of the Lord revealed in the cloud may leave us simultaneously fascinated by the cloud and perplexed by it. We have observed thus far that the cloud is a brilliant manifestation of the glory of the Lord, massive and mobile, like a burning fire shrouded by thick smoke. To be led, protected, and instructed by the cloud was to be led, protected, and instructed by the Holy Spirit. Scripture provides an awesome and mysterious depiction of this pillar in the desert. As we will now see, the Israelites had a complicated relationship with this primal revelation of God's glory, and its full significance would unfold only later in redemptive history.

God's Glory on the Move and at Rest

The cloud was often on the move. This is true in at least two important senses. On one hand, the cloud moved with respect to geography. It first appeared by the sea, through which the Israelites walked as if on dry ground; then it moved on to Sinai, and from there to various desert locales; finally, it took the Israelites to the threshold of the Promised Land, their destination.

On the other hand, the cloud moved with respect to Israel itself. The cloud appeared at varying degrees of distance and nearness to Israel as she trekked through the wilderness. The nearness of the cloud meant the presence of God. This presence of God was a sign of blessing, yet it simultaneously threatened judgment and evoked fear. The cloud brought the people into communion with the Lord, yet simultaneously excluded most of the people most of the time from intimacy with it. For the cloud to leave the Israelites would be a disaster, but for the cloud to draw too near seemed a terrifying impossibility. As we see the cloud on the move through the desert, we get the distinct sense that it was a great blessing to the Israelites,

---

4. For further discussion of the cloud and the Holy Spirit, see also Kline, *Images of the Spirit*, chap. 1.

but at the same time brought them into a relationship that was ultimately unsatisfying. As awesome as the cloud was, it demonstrated a problem more than it provided a solution. Something greater was necessary if God's glory was to be fully revealed and was truly to bless his people. As we'll see, Israel ultimately needed God's glory to be at rest, not on the move.

The cloud made its first appearance by the sea, protecting the Israelites from the Egyptian army and leading them through the waters (Exod 13–14). What happened to the cloud immediately thereafter is mysterious. While the Israelites were west of the sea, the cloud went ahead to lead them (Exod 13:21–22), but east of the sea *Moses* led them into the Desert of Shur (Exod 15:22). Not until they journey further, into the Desert of Sin, does the cloud reappear. While in this desert, the people grumbled against Moses and Aaron because they had no meat as they did during the good old days in Egypt (Exod 16:2–3). Although they aimed their complaint at Moses and Aaron, ultimately they were grumbling against God. He responded through Moses by promising to rain down manna from heaven (Exod 16:4–5): "In the evening you will know that it was the LORD who brought you out of Egypt, and in the morning you will see the glory of the LORD, because he has heard your grumbling against him" (Exod 16:6–7). And indeed they saw it: "They looked toward the desert, and there was the glory of the LORD appearing in the cloud" (Exod 16:10). Where had the cloud been? We don't know, but this text communicates a sense of distance. The people had journeyed on without the cloud and had fallen into rebellion. The glory of God in the cloud reappeared, but they only saw it from afar. Still, blessing seemed at hand: God would provide food and confirm that it was he who brought them out of Egypt.

The sense of distance did not last long. The Israelites soon made it to the Desert of Sinai and God made his presence felt as never before. Scripture now calls the cloud a "dense cloud," and the people hear God's voice speaking from within it (Exod 19:9). This is no normal cloud, for in it, "the LORD will come down on Mount Sinai in the sight of all the people" (Exod 19:11). Soon the cloud covered the mountain with smoke, accompanied by thunder, lightning, fire, an earthquake, and a trumpet blast (Exod 19:16–18).

In one sense, the distance between God and his people vanished: "Moses led the people out of the camp to meet with God, and they stood at the foot of the mountain" (Exod 19:17). But even this encounter with God communicates a strong sense of exclusion. God required Moses to put a boundary around the mountain, threatening death for anyone who even touches its foot (Exod 19:12–13, 21–24). Only Moses was able to ascend the mountain: God descended and Moses climbed and they met at "the top" (Exod 19:20). Shortly thereafter, God permitted Aaron, his sons Nadab and Abihu, and seventy elders of Israel to "come up to the LORD" (Exod 24:1), and they "saw the God of Israel," and ate and drank with him (Exod 24:10–11). But still it was Moses alone who could "approach the LORD" (Exod 24:2), accompanied by his aide Joshua (Exod 24:13). This scene ends with an awesome description that communicates both nearness and distance, intimacy (to Moses) and exclusion (for the people):

> When Moses went up on the mountain, the cloud covered it, and the glory of the LORD settled on Mount Sinai. For six days the cloud covered the mountain, and on the seventh day the LORD called to Moses from within the cloud. To the Israelites the glory of the LORD looked like a consuming fire on top of the mountain. Then Moses entered the cloud as he went on up the mountain. And he stayed on the mountain forty days and forty nights (Exod 24:15–18).

The cloud does not wait long to get back on the move, drawing yet nearer to the people but again simultaneously keeping them at a distance. After a long description of the construction of the tabernacle (Exod 26–40), the text announces that "Moses finished the work" (Exod 40:33). The Lord promised that he would "meet with the Israelites" at the entrance to the tent of meeting, and now "the cloud covered the tent of meeting, and the glory of the LORD filled the tabernacle" (Exod 40:34). This was an astounding thing, communicating the closest intimacy: the cloud that recently could be seen only far off in the wilderness has now descended into the Israelite camp and filled the tabernacle! But immediately God excludes even Moses from it: "Moses could not enter the tent of meeting because the cloud had settled on it, and the glory of the LORD filled the tabernacle" (Exod 40:35).

Shortly thereafter Aaron and his sons are ordained to priestly service and at last Israel can offer ministry in the Lord's presence: "Moses and Aaron then went into the tent of meeting. When they came out, they blessed the people and the glory of the LORD appeared to all the people. Fire came out from the presence of the LORD and consumed the burnt offering and the fat portions on the altar. And when all the people saw it, they shouted for joy and fell facedown" (Lev 9:23–24). This is a wonderful scene of God drawing near to his people in blessing. But distance and exclusion lurks even here. The people as a whole may have rejoiced at

Aaron's ministry and God's acceptance of their offerings, but they themselves were not granted access to the holy places where their priests were welcome, and not even all the priests had equal access to God's presence. As the New Testament summarizes, the priests regularly ministered in the outer room of the tabernacle, but "only the high priest entered the inner room, and that only once a year" (Heb 9:7). Even the priests could enter the tabernacle only with utmost caution. Immediately after describing the ordination and initial ministry of the priests, Leviticus relates how God strikes down Aaron's sons, Nadab and Abihu. Because they offered "unauthorized fire before the LORD," "fire came out from the presence of the LORD and consumed them" (Lev 10:1–2). The same fire from the cloud that brought joy to the people (Lev 9:23–24) brings judgment upon the disobedient (Lev 10:1–2).

Following these climactic events, the cloud keeps on moving. But now the movement again pertains to geography, as the cloud leads the people through the wilderness. Numbers 9:15 picks up the action from "the day the tabernacle, the tent of the covenant law, was set up," when "the cloud covered it." And that, the text continues, "is how it continued to be" (Num 9:16). Israel remained encamped "as long as the cloud stayed over the tabernacle" and set out whenever "the cloud lifted from above the tent." The amount of time the cloud remained at a particular location varied: it could be "for two days or a month or a year" (Num 9:17–23). One fascinating detail is that the cloud did to the tabernacle what it previously did to Sinai. It "covered" them both (cf. Exod 24:15–16). The tabernacle, covered by the cloud, was a sort of portable Sinai plodding through the desert.[5] Thus, the uneasy tension created by God simultaneously drawing near to his people yet excluding them from intimacy does not end with their departure from Sinai but accompanies them as they proceed from that holy mountain to their destination, the Promised Land.

The Blessing (?) of the Cloud

Was this moving presence of God in the cloud a blessing? What good did this revelation of the glory of the Lord do for Israel? In many respects the Old Testament leaves us hesitant to answer. On one hand, the nearness of the divine glory in the cloud was outwardly magnificent and a great gift of God to his people. On the other hand, the cloud often brought curse as

---

5.   Thanks to the Rev. Zach Keele for stimulating thoughts on this phenomenon in a sermon at Escondido Orthodox Presbyterian Church in February 2014.

well as blessing and could never be ultimately satisfying for the people of God. It's worth reflecting on both of these truths before we continue to trace the story of God's glory in the cloud after Israel's desert trek.

First, the presence of this cloud of divine glory was indeed a great testament to God's love for Israel and a sign of his favor. It is amazing to think that the one true God, eternally glorious in a way known only to himself, would reveal his glory to Israel in a magnificent cloud of smoke and fire, and through this cloud speak to them, protect them from their enemies, and make them his own covenant people! He did this for no other nation. When Aaron and his sons were ordained and began their ministry in the tabernacle enveloped by the cloud, they blessed the people, and the glory of God appeared to them all (Lev 9:22–23). In the face of such glory, and receipt of this blessing, it's no wonder that the people "shouted for joy" (Lev 9:24). Paul probably had such scenes in mind when he contemplated the wonderful gifts God had given Israel of old: "Theirs is the adoption to sonship; *theirs the divine glory*, the covenants, the receiving of the law, the temple worship and the promises" (Rom 9:4). The presence of God's glory was Israel's unique privilege. Celebrating God's goodness to Israel, the sons of Korah sang: "Surely his salvation is near those who fear him, that his glory may dwell in our land" (Ps 85:9).

One of the best ways to appreciate the blessing of the cloud's nearness is to contemplate the alternative: its absence. After Israel's shocking idolatry with the golden calf at the foot of Sinai, God threatened to send them on to the Promised Land with only an angel to lead them (Exod 33:1–3). "When the people heard these distressing words, they began to mourn" (Exod 33:4), and Moses pleaded with God to accompany them: "If your Presence does not go with us, do not send us up from here. How will anyone know that you are pleased with me and with your people unless you go with us? What else will distinguish me and your people from all the other people on the face of the earth?" (Exod 33:15–16). God mercifully relented.

Even while acknowledging Israel's great privilege in having God's glory so near, Scripture emphasizes the drawbacks and insufficiencies of his revelation through the cloud. Three examples are worth noting, all of which are evident in Exodus 33.

First, the persistent sin of God's people made the presence of his glory in their midst a major problem. The nearness of the cloud may have been the Israelites' unique privilege, but it simultaneously exposed the corruption of their hearts, and when the holiness of God approaches an unholy people, blessing quickly turns to judgment. As God explained to Moses when threatening to send them forth from Sinai alone: "I will not go with you, because you are a stiff-necked people and I might destroy you on the way" (Exod 33:3). Although the Israelites rejoiced in the presence of God's glory when their priests began ministering in the tabernacle, Israel actually trembled in fear more often than they rejoiced before his cloud of glory. In their sober moments, they realized that they had no business being so close to this glorious God. At the foot of Sinai, excluded from the mountain itself upon pain of death, they cried to Moses: "The LORD our God has shown us his glory and his majesty. . . . But now, why should we die? This great fire will consume us. . . . For what mortal has ever heard the voice of the living God speaking out of fire, as we have, and survived? Go near and listen to all that the LORD our God says. Then tell us whatever the LORD our God tells you" (Deut 5:24–27).

In their subsequent desert journey, sometimes the cloud appeared over the Tent of Meeting to bless the people, but other times it appeared there to wreak judgment upon rebels. For example, when the people refused to enter the Promised Land, and threatened to depose Moses and Aaron and appoint new leaders to take them back to Egypt, "the glory of the LORD appeared at the tent of meeting to all the Israelites" (Num 14:10) and God condemned every adult in the community (save two) to die in the wilderness. Later, in the rebellion of Korah, Dathan, and Abiram, "the glory of the LORD appeared to the entire assembly" (Num 16:19) and God announced the imminent destruction of these three and their families. When the community brazenly grumbled against Moses and Aaron after God brought this about, "suddenly the cloud covered it [the tent of meeting] and the glory of the LORD appeared" (Num 16:42), from which another plague followed. It's evident that though the Israelites despaired at the thought of God's glory leaving them, its advent usually meant trouble. Sinful Israel faced quite a predicament.

This should come as no surprise to anyone acquainted with broader biblical teachings on divine holiness and human sinfulness. To be confronted with God's revelation brings responsibility, and disobedience provokes judgment. Every person, simply by virtue of living in this world, is confronted by God's revelation in nature and is therefore liable before him (Rom 1:18–20). How much more, then, were God's Old Testament people accountable to him when he made his glory visible to them in such striking ways? As God said to Israel, "not one of those who saw my glory and the signs I performed in Egypt and in the wilderness but who disobeyed me and tested me ten times—not one of them will ever see the land I promised on oath to their ancestors. No one who has treated me with contempt will ever see it" (Num 14:22–23).

We may shudder to think of beholding the great glory of the Lord and then treating him with contempt, yet this was precisely the Israelites' downfall. What did they do at Sinai but "exchange their glorious God [literally, 'their glory'] for an image of a bull, which eats grass" (Ps 106:20)? And it only became worse: Jeremiah uses similar language to describe Israel's exchange of God's glory for "worthless idols" (Jer 2:11; cf. Hos 4:7). Shocking? Jeremiah thought so: "Be appalled at this, you heavens, and shudder with great horror" (Jer 2:12). Isaiah adds: "Jerusalem staggers, Judah is falling; their words and deeds are against the LORD, defying his glorious presence" (Isa 3:8). Confronted with God's glory, sinners' rebellion becomes all the more heinous and worthy of judgment. As Jesus would later put it: "From everyone who has been given much, much will be demanded; and from the one who has been entrusted with much, much more will be asked" (Luke 12:48). Paul's description of Moses' work, therefore, makes perfect sense. His was a ministry that "came with glory," yet it brought "death" and "condemnation" (2 Cor 3:7–11).

The drawbacks and limitations of this revelation of God's glory also appear in the fact that the cloud was regularly on the move. The cloud's mobility may have contributed to its magnificence, but it surely did not promote Israel's spiritual peace. Numbers 9:17–23 is interesting in this regard. With a degree of detail that seems a bit repetitive and almost pedantic, the text describes the cloud settling, then moving, settling, then moving. The Israelites, following the cloud's lead, camp, then set out, camp, then set out. Why does Scripture labor over these details? In part, it creates an impression of uprootedness. The Israelites have no stable home, no lasting place to lay their heads. The cloud would sometimes stay at a place for only one day—but then sometimes two days, a month, or a year (Num 14:21–22), and apparently Israel didn't know in advance. The whole point of the wilderness travel was to reach the Promised Land. God set his Presence among them in order to give them "rest" (Exod 33:14). But in the desert they had no rest, only unpredictable movement. They could only look ahead and hope for something better in the future.

Finally, Scripture indicates the limitations of the cloud's revelation of God's glory by describing Moses' dissatisfaction with what he saw (Exod 33:18–33). This is initially a surprising account. Previous chapters in Exodus recount how the majestic cloud covered Sinai and how Moses entered the cloud at the top of the mountain, received the law from God, and remained there for forty days and nights. It seems safe to surmise that Moses experienced an intimacy with God unsurpassed in human history to that point. God may have spoken to other prophets through visions and dreams, but with Moses he spoke "face to face;" Moses saw "the form of the LORD" (Num 12:6–8). But then, almost immediately after that incredible experience, Moses says to God: "Now show me your glory" (Exod 33:18). We almost fear that God will strike Moses down for presumption. But he does nothing of the sort. His reply contains no hint of rebuke. God tells Moses: "I will cause all my goodness to pass in front of you, and I will proclaim my name, the LORD, in your presence. . . . But . . . you cannot see my face, for no one may see me and live" (Exod 33:19–20). Then God directs Moses to a certain place and says: "When my glory passes by, I will put you in a cleft in the rock and cover you with my hand until I have passed by. Then I will remove my hand and you will see my back; but my face must not be seen" (Exod 33:22–23).

This is all highly mysterious. Had not Moses been in the cloud, in the intimate presence of God's glory, for many weeks? Wasn't he the man with whom God actually did speak face to face? A precise explanation eludes us. What is clear, however, is that Moses came to realize that as awesome as God's glory in the cloud may have appeared, the full glory of God actually far surpassed it. Moses enjoyed quite a taste of God's glory, but recognized that it was only an appetizer. The "glory" and "face" of God that he saw at the top of Sinai was, from another perspective, not even the equivalent of seeing God's "back." This "man of God" (cf. Deut 33:1) rightly desired even greater communion with his Lord.[6] Once again we see that a glory even better—far better—than what the cloud revealed must be in Israel's future.

It's worth reflecting for a moment on New Testament teaching. Hebrews 9 makes it clear that God intentionally designed the cloud-crowned tabernacle to signal incompleteness and insufficiency. By the fact that only the high priest could enter the inner sanctuary, and only once a year (thus indicating that the cloud excluded even as it drew near), "the

---

6.   John Calvin viewed Moses' request somewhat differently. He writes that Moses was "carried beyond due bounds, and longs for more than is lawful or expedient," and thus adds that this text should "act as a restraint upon us, to repress the speculations which are too wild and wanton in us." See John Calvin, *Calvin's Commentaries*, vol. 3 (Grand Rapids: Baker, 2003), 377. Calvin's concern about not speculating about God's nature beyond what is lawful is well taken, but I do not think it is clear from the text that this is what Moses was doing. In any case, Moses' request still demonstrates that God's revelation in the cloud was not ultimately satisfying.

Holy Spirit was showing . . . that the way into the Most Holy Place had not yet been disclosed as long as the first tabernacle was still functioning." The gifts and sacrifices offered in that tabernacle "were not able to clear the conscience of the worshiper" (that is, the cloud in the desert did not truly atone for the people's sin). These were "external regulations applying until the time of the new order" (Heb 9:7–10). The glory of God in the cloud was awesome, but a greater glory, with greater and unshakable blessing for the people of God, was yet to come.

God's Glory in the Promised Land

The glory of God revealed in the cloud was on a journey, and after forty long years that journey finally came to an end. Israel entered the Promised Land under Joshua. Scripture never presents a farewell scene for the cloud that led the Israelites during their trek. Instead the cloud quietly drops from readers' view, and we are left presuming that the cloud dropped from physical view around the time Israel's host crossed the Jordan River. And so we wonder: was that greater experience of God's glory achieved once they reached the Promised Land?

It was in part. Although the Israelites no longer saw the outward magnificence of the cloud as they saw it in the wilderness, in the Promised Land God did reveal his glory and grant his people communion with that glory in certain ways that transcended their experience while on the move. At the same time, the drawbacks and limitations observed above continued to haunt the Israelites. Their sin still disqualified them as communicants with God's glory and they lacked the stable and sure access to God's presence that weak creatures so desperately need. The story of God's glory with the Israelites in the Land, so impressive and promising at times, turned into major tragedy and left them still longing for something far better.

Although the pillar of cloud and fire disappears as the people settle throughout the Promised Land, Israel continues to regard the tabernacle as the place where God's glory dwells, particularly because it houses the ark of the covenant. Consider 1 Samuel 4, which recounts the debacle in which Israelite soldiers recklessly grabbed the ark from its provisional home in Shiloh to use as a talisman in battle against the Philistines, who promptly routed the Israelites and captured the ark. Upon hearing this news, the daughter-in-law of Eli the priest named her newborn son "Ichabod," which means "without glory." With her dying breath "she said, 'The Glory has departed from Israel, for the ark of God has been captured'" (1 Sam

4:21–22). Some years later, presumably after the ark and tabernacle had been moved to Jerusalem, David sings, "LORD, I love the house where you live, the place where your glory dwells" (Ps 26:8); elsewhere he writes, "I have seen you in the sanctuary and beheld your power and your glory" (Ps 63:2). How did David "see" God and "behold" his glory? Scripture never describes a visible, cloud-like manifestation of God's glory during this period in Israel's history, so David, it seems, perceived the presence of God in the tabernacle, whose innermost room contained both the ark, symbolizing the footstool of God, and the cherubim figures, representing the angelic host surrounding his heavenly throne.[7]

Soon thereafter, God's visible glory made a triumphant return. David wished to build a temple to provide God's presence with a permanent location in Jerusalem. God did not permit him to do so, but commissioned his son Solomon to build a magnificent structure and to bring the trappings of the tabernacle into this stately house. First Kings 8 and 2 Chronicles 5–7 describe the ark's entrance into the temple and the celebratory worship that follows. Something strikingly familiar takes place after the priests put the ark in place: "When the priests withdrew from the Holy Place, the cloud filled the temple of the LORD. And the priests could not perform their service because of the cloud, for the glory of the LORD filled his temple" (1 Kgs 8:10–11; 2 Chr 5:13–14). Then, after Solomon blessed the people and offered a prayer of dedication, "fire came down from heaven and consumed the burnt offering and the sacrifices, and the glory of the LORD filled it. . . . When all the Israelites saw the fire coming down and the glory of the LORD above the temple, they knelt on the pavement with their faces to the ground, and they worshiped and gave thanks to the LORD" (2 Chr 7:1–3). This scene in the new temple replicates the events under Moses and Aaron after the construction of the original tabernacle (Exod 40; Lev 9). "A glorious throne," said Jeremiah, "is the place of our sanctuary" (Jer 17:12).

In at least one important way, the temple constituted a greater blessing than any the Israelites had yet experienced. One of the deficiencies of their experience in the wilderness was that the cloud—and hence the tabernacle—remained on the move. Their camps were always temporary,

---

7.   G. K. Beale calls upon another interesting piece of evidence to support a similar claim in *The Temple and the Church's Mission: A Biblical Theology of the Dwelling Place of God* (Downers Grove, IL: Intervarsity, 2004), 66. He writes: "Israel's temple was the place where the priest experienced God's unique presence, and Eden was the place where Adam walked and talked with God. The same Hebrew verbal form . . . used for God's 'walking back and forth' in the Garden (Gen. 3:8), also describes God's presence in the tabernacle (Lev. 26:12; Deut. 23:14 [15]; 2 Sam. 7:6–7)."

their life always transient. Even after they entered the Promised Land, the ark continued to move around in an often unsavory saga (e.g., 1 Sam 4–6; 2 Sam 6). Now, it finally came to rest. Solomon prayed: "Arise, LORD God, and come to your resting place, you and the ark of your might" (2 Chr 6:41). The journey from Mount Sinai at last ends at Mount Zion. Presumably the cloud itself did not remain permanently visible in the temple, but it does seem that here, at last, God's glory dwells with his people in stability and security.[8]

But some things never change. The Israelites will come to realize again that God's glory is far greater than they can comprehend, and even moments of blessing and joy at the nearness of God's glory fade into terrible disappointment. Even with God's glory seemingly at rest on Zion, stability and security remain elusive.

The prophets' experience perhaps best displays that the glory of God is far more awesome than even the scene at the dedication of the temple revealed. One of the things that distinguishes a prophet from the rest of God's people is that he stands "in the council of the LORD to see [and] to hear his word" (Jer 23:18). Where is this council of God if not where he sits enthroned surrounded by his angelic host? And where does he sit enthroned surrounded by his angelic host if not in heaven itself? And where is this heavenly council manifest on earth if not in the cloud? When God's Old Testament prophets entered "the council of the LORD," they were apparently taken into the midst of the cloud (as only Moses, the great prophet, had experienced before) and there given a glimpse of heavenly glory.[9]

Consider Isaiah's dramatic call to the prophetic ministry. He sees the train of God's robe filling "the temple," but this is clearly not the temple in Jerusalem. For the Lord is "high and exalted, seated on a throne," and "above him were seraphim, each with six wings: With two wings they covered their faces, with two they covered their feet, and with two they were flying. And they were calling to one another: 'Holy, holy, holy is the LORD Almighty; the whole earth is full of his glory.' At the sound of their voices, the doorposts and thresholds shook and the temple was filled with smoke" (Isa 6:1–4). Glory, smoke, angels, and God enthroned—all of this is imagery of the pillar of cloud and fire we considered above.

Ezekiel, too, saw extraordinary things when God commissioned him as a prophet. When the hand of the Lord comes upon him, Ezekiel records, "I looked, and I saw a windstorm coming out of the north—an immense

---

8. On the relationship of the temple to divine "rest," see also Beale, *The Temple*, 60–66.
9. For further discussion of this point, see also Kline, *Images of the Spirit*, 57–64.

cloud with flashing lightning and surrounded by brilliant light. The center of the fire looked like glowing metal, and in the fire was what looked like four living creatures" (Ezek 1:3–5). Again, the cloud appears with many of its accompanying features: lightning, fire, and angels (the living creatures are later identified as cherubim: Ezek 10:15). Later he sees a throne, and a "figure like that of a man" seated upon it (Ezek 1:26). Ezekiel concludes the account of his first vision thus: "Like the appearance of a rainbow in the clouds on a rainy day, so was the radiance around him. This was the appearance of the likeness of the glory of the LORD" (Ezek 1:28). Later he sees "the glory of the LORD" again (Ezek 3:12, 23).

These texts indicate that Isaiah and Ezekiel immediately realized they had seen something utterly astounding, visions that far surpassed their experience of God's glory in the ordinary temple ministry. Isaiah cries out, "Woe to me . . . I am ruined" (Isa 6:5), and Ezekiel falls facedown (Ezek 1:28). Through supernatural visions they entered the cloud of glory and were thereby admitted into the "council of the LORD" (Jer 23:18). Surely these prophets would never again suspect that the glory of God in the temple was anything but a faint reflection of the divine glory in full splendor.

God's glory in the temple was ultimately unsatisfying not only because it afforded a clouded glimpse of his full majesty, but also because it could not abide with a sinful people. The same problem the Israelites experienced in the wilderness recurred generation after generation in the Promised Land. The presence of God's glory originally seems to be a blessing, but the holy glory of God and the despicable sin of the people prove to be fundamentally incompatible. This explains Isaiah's reaction to seeing God in the cloud. He cries out, "Woe to me" because "I am a man of unclean lips, and I live among a people of unclean lips, and my eyes have seen the King, the LORD Almighty" (Isa 6:5). Isaiah's immediate instinct when confronted with the glory of the Lord is to feel the horrible burden of his sin.

For many years the Lord was merciful to his repeatedly rebellious people. He often brought minor judgments upon them but held back the full brunt of his wrath. Nevertheless, the law of Moses threatened more than just minor judgments. It threatened exile from the Land (e.g., Lev 18:26–28; Deut 28:63–68). Moses, in fact, told the people prior to entering the Land that all of the law's curses would inevitably rise upon them (Deut 30:1). And so at last, God not only scattered the northern ten tribes at the hand of Assyria but also sent the ruthless Babylonians against Judah and Jerusalem to dethrone their king, destroy the temple, and haul most of the survivors off to exile in Babylon.

Ezekiel had the unenviable privilege of seeing this devastating judgment for what it really was: God abandoning his people as his glory departed from Israel. In a series of visions, Ezekiel was first taken to the temple court in Jerusalem, where he saw "the glory of the God of Israel" (Ezek 8:4), as in his vision of the cloud described above. Through the rest of the chapter God shows Ezekiel all the wretched idolatry transpiring around the temple. The visions continue in the next chapter, which begins with God calling six armed men to execute judgment (Ezek 9:1–2). Ezekiel writes: "Now the glory of the God of Israel went up from above the cherubim, where it had been, and moved to the threshold of the temple" (Ezek 9:3). In the days of Solomon, God's glory in the cloud settled upon the temple as its resting place, but here it arises and ominously begins to move again. Shortly thereafter, Ezekiel looks and beholds "the likeness of a throne of lapis lazuli above the vault that was over the heads of the cherubim" (Ezek 10:1). Then "the glory of the LORD rose from above the cherubim and moved to the threshold of the temple. The cloud filled the temple, and the court was full of the radiance of the glory of the LORD" (Ezek 10:4). Ezekiel also sees cherubim (the "living creatures" of his original vision), which rise upward (Ezek 10:15). Finally, he reports, "the glory of the LORD departed from over the threshold of the temple and stopped above the cherubim. While I watched, the cherubim spread their wings and rose from the ground. . . . They stopped at the entrance of the east gate of the LORD's house, and the glory of the God of Israel was above them" (Ezek 10:18–19).

Invisible to the naked eye, in other words, the exile was preceded by the most dreadful of events: the glory of the Lord departed from the temple. The glorious cloud that came to rest on the tabernacle (Exod 40:34–35) and later the temple (1 Kgs 8:10–12) got up and left. What looked to be stable and sure proved to be nothing of the sort. The hoped-for resting place of the ark would soon be decimated. What Moses feared in the wilderness had finally come to pass: the glory of the Lord abandoned his sinful people. The Israelites could not live the righteous life required of those dwelling in God's presence, and their temple sacrifices could not sufficiently atone for sin. God cast the polluted people away from his holy glory.

Conclusion

The story of God's glory narrated thus far is sobering, puzzling, and even disappointing. What seemed so majestic—that pillar of cloud and fire inhabited by God himself, seated upon his throne and surrounded by the angelic host—ends up being repulsed by his people's rebellion and thus, it deserts them, leaving them in misery at the hands of their enemies.

Who can read this Old Testament history and not proclaim *soli Deo gloria*? Page after page shows that all glory belongs to God alone. Especially evident is that God glorifies himself through his judgment upon the unrighteous. Not so clear, however, is the Reformation's related claim that God glorifies himself in part by glorifying his people, such that *soli Deo gloria* becomes part of the good news of salvation. At the time of Israel's exile, this seemed very far from the truth. How could this majestically holy God glorify himself except by *judging* his persistently sinful people? How glad we are that the story of God's glory does not end with the exile. Later Old Testament books prophesy the return of divine glory to Israel, and the New Testament announces the coming of one who does indeed make *soli Deo gloria* a message of good news for God's people.

CHAPTER 4

The Brightness of His Father's Glory: The Glory of God Incarnate

"Suddenly a great company of the heavenly host appeared with the angel, praising God and saying, 'Glory to God in the highest heaven, and on earth peace to those on whom his favor rests.'"
—*Luke 2:13–14*

The "rulers of this age . . . crucified the Lord of glory."
—*1 Corinthians 2:8*

The Lord is a God of great glory. Internally glorious in ways known only to himself, he also reveals his glory in this world and through this world, and he glorifies himself in all his works. These great truths of *soli Deo gloria* are abundantly clear in the Old Testament story traced in the previous chapter. Although the Old Testament speaks of God's glory in a variety of ways, it gives special attention to its revelation in the pillar of cloud and fire, first during Israel's wilderness wanderings and then in its coming to rest in the temple.

A Discouraging Story So Far

This Old Testament storyline, however, was in many respects more discouraging than encouraging. Not only did God occasionally remind the Israelites that his glory far transcends what they had seen and experienced, but he also constantly reminded them that their persistent sinful rebellion was fundamentally incompatible with the blessed communion that the approach of the glorious cloud seemed to promise. It was often more than reminder. Many times in the desert, the glory of the Lord brought judgment against the recalcitrant, and at the end of the story recounted in Chapter 3, God's glory actually departed from Israel, rising from its resting place in the inner sanctuary of the temple and leaving Jerusalem to the fury of the Babylonians. Yet where we left off was not the end of the Old Testament story. Later Old Testament prophets speak of a glory yet to come. The glory of the Lord would not only return to Israel, but far surpass it in majesty and in blessing for God's people.

When we hear this, we may still wonder if there's any reason to think things will turn out better after the return from exile. God had shown the Israelites mercy many times and given them progressively greater revelations of his glory, but to no lasting avail since Israel remained stubbornly disobedient. Nevertheless, this time *is* different. It is different because God now reveals his greater glory, and indeed his greatest glory, not in a mobile cloud or an earthly temple but in his own Son, the promised Messiah. As we now recognize in hindsight, this Son, "the radiance of God's glory" (Heb 1:3), who possessed "the Spirit without limit" (John 3:34), not only reveals the glory of God in a surprising, unique, and final way, but also resolves the seemingly unsolvable problem of sin. He justifies, sanctifies, and glorifies God's people that they might glorify and enjoy him forever, without any specter of judgment. Christ is the true glory of God who draws near to his people, never to depart.

These great truths are the focus of Chapters 4 and 5. Here in Chapter 4, we examine the supreme yet unexpected revelation of God's glory in his Son, the Lord Jesus Christ. In Chapter 5, we will turn to the good news of how we, his people, are swept up into this story and so made able to glorify him and to share in his heavenly glory for ages everlasting.

After the Exile: The Return of God's Glory

The previous chapter ended in the dark night of exile. Anyone who reads the book of Lamentations gains an acute appreciation of just how traumatic the destruction of Jerusalem was and just how desolate it left its survivors. God's glory had departed, and the Lord was silent. The Israelites could not abide the presence of God's glory, but what hope did they have in its absence? What expectations remained for the future?

When the Israelites regained their composure, they could have found the answer already in their midst. Some of the same prophets who predicted the advent of exile also provided resources to arm them with encouragement once that terrible event transpired, and several subsequent prophets would reinforce their message. The good news of comfort often took a form unsurprising in light of Israel's prior history: the glory of God would return to his people in a rebuilt Jerusalem with its rebuilt temple. But this time his glory would also draw the nations of the world to its light and not be satisfied until redeemed people from all the earth were gathered in a heavenly temple that far surpasses any structure built by human hands.

Israel in exile could begin finding hope by turning back to one of her pre-exilic prophets, Isaiah, and hearing his description of God's people banished again to the desert but ransomed by the Lord, who would make the desert bloom before them and build them a highway back to Zion, which they would enter with gladness and everlasting joy (Isa 35). Even there in the desert "they will see the glory of the LORD, the splendor of our God" (Isa 35:2). The glory of God's presence would accompany their re-entrance into the Promised Land from the wilderness, as it did their first entrance. The opening of Isaiah 40 famously describes a similar scene, a highway through the desert leading back to Jerusalem. On this superhigh-way, before which mountains are leveled and valleys raised, "the glory of the LORD will be revealed, and all people will see it together" (Isa 40:5).

But what would they find when they returned to Jerusalem? Isaiah prophesied of a coming day in which the land and its people would be cleansed (Isa 4:2–4). At that time, "the LORD will create over all of Mount Zion and over those who assemble there a cloud of smoke by day and a glow of flaming fire by night; over everything the glory will be a canopy. It will be a shelter and shade from the heat of the day, and a refuge and hiding place from the storm and rain" (Isa 4:5–6). This description bor-rows the language of the pillar of cloud and fire that had accompanied the Israelites on their first wilderness trek and had come to rest upon the first temple, but it also suggests something even better to come. This time the cloud would cover the entire city and form a dome of protection from the elements. Ezekiel's account of a new, post-exilic temple is even more magnificent, comprising the last nine chapters of his prophecy. In this account he writes, "I saw the glory of the God of Israel coming from the east. His voice was like the roar of rushing waters, and the land was radiant with his glory. The vision I saw was like the vision I had seen when he came to destroy the city and like the visions I had seen by the Kebar River [discussed in Chapter 3], and I fell facedown. The glory of the LORD entered the temple through the gate facing east. Then the Spirit lifted me up and brought me into the inner court, and the glory of the LORD filled the temple" (Ezek 43:2–5; cf. 44:4).

When the Israelites did return to Jerusalem, the prophets of that day urged them to set to work restoring the city and its new temple, with words that again promised the return of divine glory. Zechariah records the words of an angel, who shares this message from God: "'Jerusalem will be a city without walls because of the great number of people and animals in it. And I myself will be a wall of fire around it,' declares the LORD, 'and I will be its glory within'" (Zech 2:5). Through Haggai, God promises that "in a little while" he will "shake all nations, and what is desired by all nations will come, and I will fill this house with glory, says the LORD Almighty . . . The glory of this present house will be greater than the glory of the former house,' says the LORD Almighty. 'And in this place I will grant peace" (Hag 2:7, 9).

A remarkable feature of the coming glory is that it accompanies the one "desired by *all nations.*" The coming glory, Haggai thus indicates, will not be for Israel alone. This is another theme Isaiah addresses, sometimes with memorable eloquence: "Arise, shine, for your light has come, and the glory of the LORD rises upon you. See, darkness covers the earth and thick darkness is over the peoples, but the LORD rises upon you and his glory appears over you. Nations will come to your light, and kings to the brightness of your dawn" (Isa 60:3). He says later concerning Jerusalem, "The nations will see your vindication, and all kings your glory" (Isa 62:2). Near the end of his prophecy, Isaiah adds: "I will send some of those who survive to the nations—to Tarshish, to the Libyans and Lydians . . . to Tubal and Greece, and to the distant islands that have not heard of my fame or seen my glory. They will proclaim my glory among the nations" (Isa 66:19).

We need to be clear that the prophets were not speaking merely (or even primarily) about the Israelites' experience in the Promised Land or the new temple building they constructed after their return from exile. The glory of that building never did in fact exceed that of the former, and the nations never flocked to Jerusalem to see it. In these prophecies God was directing his people to something far, far greater, a reality to which the second temple in Jerusalem could only point dimly.

For example, Isaiah spoke of many nations seeing God's glory (Isa 66:19) in conjunction with the advent of "new heavens and a new earth" in which "the former things will not be remembered" (Isa 65:17–18; cf. 66:22). Furthermore, Ezekiel's magnificent account of a new temple adorned with divine glory (Ezek 40–48) described specifications for its structure, geographical division of the surrounding land, and even a spectacular river originating from the temple, all of which make clear that he pointed to something far transcending the second temple or the earthly Jerusalem and its environs. Like Isaiah, Ezekiel saw visions of new heavens and a new earth. But perhaps most important is an easily missed detail from Haggai 2. Haggai looked forward to a coming day when God would send the one "desired by all nations" (Hag 2:7). This can be none other than the Messiah. The Israelites needed to set their sights upon something much greater than a new temple their own hands would build. They needed to look for the promised Savior of all nations and for the new heavens and new earth that he would bring. Only through these gifts, the Old Testament prophets indicate, would God's greater glory come to bless Israel and all the world.

Thus, the Israelites had good reason to hope even in the midst of their degrading exile. To pursue our storyline and to see how God has fulfilled these promises, we must now consider this Messiah and his new creation kingdom.

The Promised Messiah, King of Glory

The question that looms as we contemplate Israel in exile and the amazing promises of future glory is how things could possibly work out better next time. What exactly will change to prevent the seemingly inevitable clash between God's holy glory and his people's deep-seated sin? The answer is that this time, the glory of the Lord will be revealed in his Son, the promised Messiah. His greater revelation of divine glory will reconcile God and his people and enable them to experience the presence of that glory fully as a blessing and not as a curse. *Soli Deo gloria* becomes part and parcel of the gospel through the Lord Jesus Christ.

Even as the Old Testament prophesied a greater dawn of divine glory in a restored temple in Jerusalem, so it also prophesied a coming Messiah to accompany them. God established David's line to rule over Israel forever (2 Sam 7:12–16), and David acknowledged the glory God had bestowed on his house: "Through the victories you gave, his [the king's] glory is great; you have bestowed on him splendor and majesty" (Ps 21:5). The fortunes of David's line, however, matched those of the old temple. As Kings and Chronicles recount, David's royal descendants were a sorry lot, the best of them plagued by folly and the worst of them scandalous idolaters. Rather than representing the people righteously before God and delivering them from their enemies, they regularly provoked God's wrath and fell before foreign oppressors. David's house seemed to meet the same ignoble end as that of the old temple in Jerusalem. When conquering the land and destroying the temple, the Babylonians unseated David's descendants and left his throne vacant.

But as the fortunes of David's line declined along with those of the old city and temple, so would they be revived with the new city and temple. The beautiful prophecy in Isaiah 4, describing the pillar of cloud and fire as a canopy of glory over all of Mount Zion, begins with a corresponding promise about the messianic king: "In that day the Branch of the LORD will be beautiful and glorious" (Isa 4:2). Shortly thereafter, Isaiah speaks of similar themes and makes explicit that this Branch is indeed the offspring of David: "A shoot will come up from the stump of Jesse; from his roots a branch will bear fruit" (Isa 11:1), and "In that day the Root of Jesse will stand as a banner for the peoples; the nations will rally to him, and his resting place will be glorious" (Isa 11:10). No wonder John later wrote that Isaiah "saw Jesus' glory and spoke about him" (John 12:41). Isaiah 11, in fact, makes clear that the coming of the Messiah, David's son, corresponds to those other great future events we considered earlier. With the coming of the king, the Lord draws the nations to himself along with Israel (Isa 11:10–12) and ushers in a new order of creation marked by universal righteousness and peace (Isa 11:4–9; cf. Hab 2:14). Here is further confirmation that God wished the Israelites to look far beyond their experience of rebuilding Jerusalem and its temple upon return from exile. God's glory would be fully displayed, for the unmitigated comfort of his people, only with the coming of the Messiah and his new creation kingdom.

After Christ's cross and resurrection, the New Testament writers speak of him as the Old Testament prophets did, as the one through whom God supremely reveals his glory. He is "the radiance of God's glory and the exact representation of his being" (Heb 1:3). "The word became flesh and made his dwelling among us. We have seen his glory, the glory of the one and only Son, who came from the Father, full of grace and truth" (John 1:14). He is "the Lord of glory" (1 Cor 2:8) or, more expansively, "our glorious Lord Jesus Christ" (Jas 2:1). "The light of the gospel," writes Paul, "displays the glory of Christ, who is the image of God" (2 Cor 4:4).

As the story of God's glory progresses, therefore, attention shifts from the pillar of cloud and fire to the coming Messiah. Should we be puzzled by this? Does the story get off track and lose its organic continuity? This chapter and the next explore many ways in which these two themes—the cloud of glory and the Lord Jesus Christ—really constitute one grand story of God glorifying himself in this world and the next. Here are a few initial ideas to illumine this truth.

The first concerns Jesus as the true and ultimate temple of God. In the Old Testament, God made his glory dwell in Solomon's temple through the cloud. Scripture therefore called the temple the place of God's dwelling, the place that bore his name (e.g., 1 Kgs 8:29; cf. Exod 29:42–46). But Jesus came as *the* dwelling of God among men, the brightest revelation of divine glory (John 1:14). His name was Immanuel, "God with us" (Matt 1:23). Hence Jesus referred to his very body as "the temple," a reference his disciples comprehended only after the resurrection (John 2:19–22). Jesus' advent meant no more need for a temple (see John 4:21), because God's supremely glorious presence in Jesus so far surpassed the most impressive glory of any earthly structure.[1] This is why the new heaven and new earth—where we might most expect to find one—will have no temple: "because the Lord God Almighty and the Lamb are its temple"; indeed, "the glory of God gives it light, and the Lamb is its lamp" (Rev 21:22–23). The glory of God revealed in Christ is thus precisely what the glory of the cloud resting upon the Old Testament temple foresignified.

Second, the themes of cloud and coming Messiah are unified through the work of the Holy Spirit. In the previous chapter, I noted how the Old Testament associated the Spirit with the cloud. In a mysterious revelation of the holy Trinity, the Old Testament portrayed God as enthroned at the center of the cloud while describing the cloud itself as a manifestation of his Spirit leading Israel through the wilderness. Although the Old Testament speaks relatively infrequently about the Spirit, it both associates him explicitly with the cloud and links him explicitly to the coming Messiah. The Spirit would rest upon Christ as the Spirit rested upon the tabernacle and temple through the cloud.

Isaiah makes the grandest of these promises. On the day the glorious Branch of the Lord arises and the cloud of smoke and fire forms a canopy over Zion, he writes, God will "cleanse the bloodstains from Jerusalem by the Spirit of judgment and the Spirit of fire" (Isa 4:4).[2] When the shoot comes up from the stump of Jesse and the Branch bears fruit from his roots, "the Spirit of the LORD will rest on him—the Spirit of wisdom and of understanding, the Spirit of counsel and of might, the Spirit of the knowledge and fear of the LORD" (Isa 11:1–2). Later, in Isaiah's famous "servant songs" about the coming Messiah, God declares: "Here is my servant, whom I uphold, my chosen one in whom I delight; I will put my Spirit on him, and he will bring justice to the nations" (Isa 42:1). Finally,

---

1. For further discussion of Jesus as the true temple in John, see G. K. Beale, *The Temple and the Church's Mission: A Biblical Theology of the Dwelling Place of God* (Downers Grove, IL: InterVarsity Press, 2004), 192–200.

2. I use the alternative NIV translation, which twice substitutes "the Spirit" for "a spirit," which I regard as much more plausible.

Isaiah writes: "The Spirit of the Sovereign LORD is upon me, because the LORD has anointed me" (Isa 61:1)—and Jesus borrowed these words to describe his ministry (Luke 4:17–21). Indeed, throughout Isaiah one of the primary characteristics of the coming Messiah is that he would be filled with the Holy Spirit, as was the temple of old through the cloud.

The New Testament embraces this theme and demonstrates that Jesus is the Christ by portraying him as Spirit-empowered.[3] He was conceived by the Spirit in Mary's womb (Luke 1:35). He fulfilled the prophecies in Isaiah considered above (Matt 12:17–21; Luke 4:17–21). He was baptized with the Holy Spirit (Matt 3:16; Mark 1:10; Luke 3:22; Acts 10:37–38) and he baptizes others with the Holy Spirit (Matt 3:11; Mark 1:8; Luke 3:16; John 1:34). The Spirit drove Jesus out into the wilderness to be tempted (Mark 1:12) and by the Spirit, Jesus later drove out demons (Matt 12:28; Mark 1:34). Jesus rejoiced by the Spirit in his conquest over these demonic powers (Luke 10:21). At the end of his life, "through the eternal Spirit [Christ] offered himself unblemished to God" (Heb 9:14). God indeed gave him the Spirit without measure (John 3:34).

Later in this chapter we will see how the Spirit remains active in Christ's resurrection and ascension. What's important to note now is that just as the story of God's glory in the cloud was simultaneously the story of God's Spirit, so also the story of God's glory in Christ is simultaneously the story of God's Spirit. The shift in focus from God's glory revealed in the pillar of cloud and fire to God's glory revealed in his Son occurs as part of one organically connected story that the Holy Spirit binds together as a unified whole.

The Messiah's Glory—or Humiliation?

Some of the straightforward assertions about Christ's glory noted above may obscure the fact that the New Testament's presentation of this theme is anything but prosaic. Before going any further in our study of Christ's glory, we need to consider one of the most profound aspects of Christ's incarnation and work, initially puzzling yet absolutely crucial for understanding both his ministry and the Christian faith and life to which we're called. I refer to the astounding reality that "the radiance of God's

---

3. For additional discussion of this point, see Sinclair B. Ferguson, *The Holy Spirit* (Downers Grove, IL: InterVarsity Press, 1996), chap. 2; and Herman Bavinck, *Reformed Dogmatics*, vol. 3, *Sin and Salvation in Christ*, ed. John Bolt, trans. John Vriend (Grand Rapids: Baker Academic, 2006), 498–503, 571–72.

glory" (Heb 1:3) appeared to this world in abject humility—as a human being, "in a low condition."[4]

It is striking and deeply important that the climactic revelation of God's glory took place *in and through a human being*. Who would have dared to imagine that, after endless generations of God's glory in the cloud drawing near and then being repelled by rebellious human beings, the glory of God would appear as a man? Yet in his inscrutable wisdom, God willed to reconcile his people to himself by sending his Son as divine glory in human flesh. Here a theme in Reformed Orthodox theology begins coming into biblical focus. God chooses to glorify himself in and through human beings, first and foremost through his own Son become man, but also through his chosen people called to share his glory in union with Christ.

What is profound is not just that Christ, the image of God's glory, became man, but that he came to share humanity's miserable condition. He himself had no sin (2 Cor 5:21; Heb 4:15), but God sent him "in the likeness of sinful flesh to be a sin offering" (Rom 8:3). Isaiah's servant songs portrayed the coming Messiah as crowned by the Spirit, but these songs also declare that many "were appalled at him—his appearance was so disfigured beyond that of any human being and his form marred beyond human likeness" (Isa 52:14). The glory of God dwelled among us, yet "he had no beauty or majesty to attract us to him, nothing in his appearance that we should desire him. . . . Like one from whom people hide their faces he was despised, and we held him in low esteem" (Isa 53:2–3). Paul calls Christ the "Lord of glory," indeed, but only to point out the awful fact that the "rulers of this age . . . *crucified* the Lord of glory" (1 Cor 2:8).

Human language fails us as we try to describe this supreme paradox, the divine glory manifest in profound humility. It is a truth that faith believes and tongue confesses more than mind understands. Yet this truth is central to the dynamic of the gospels' story. God will only bring the story of his glory to its climactic goal through the deep valley of his Son's humiliation. As considered in Chapter 1, Martin Luther remarked: "It is not sufficient for anyone, and it does him no good to recognize God in his glory and majesty, unless he recognizes him in the humility and shame of the cross."[5] This dynamic defines our own experience as Christian believers. As we'll ponder at length in Chapter 5, even now God is transforming

---

4.   *Westminster Shorter Catechism*, 27.
5.   Martin Luther, *Luther's Works*, vol. 31, *Career of the Reformer: I*, ed. Harold J. Grimm, gen. ed. Helmut T. Lehmann (Philadelphia: Fortress, 1957), 52.

us "from glory unto glory"[6] (2 Cor 3:18), yet at the same time God calls us to "share in his sufferings in order that we may also share in his glory," "the glory that will be revealed in us" (Rom 8:17–18).

The Glory and Humility of Christ's Earthly Ministry

As we now seek to follow the story of God's glory through Christ's earthly ministry, we should be attentive to this paradoxical theme of glory revealed in humility.[7] This theme emerges immediately, in fact, in the well-known account of Jesus' birth. On the night of Mary's delivery, a band of shepherds nearby had an unforgettable experience: "An angel of the Lord appeared to them, and the glory of the Lord shone around them" (Luke 2:9)—a scene that reminds us of the Old Testament cloud. The shepherds reacted as Isaiah and Ezekiel did: "they were terrified" (Luke 2:9). The angel's message began gloriously. He announced good news of "great joy for all the people," for in the city of David, a Savior was born, "the Messiah, the Lord" (Luke 2:10–11). So many wonderful Old Testament promises seem to converge in this taut proclamation. But the angel also gives the shepherds a sign, and though it sounds so familiar to those who have heard this story many times, it may have struck the shepherds as fairly underwhelming: "You will find a baby wrapped in cloths and lying in a manger" (Luke 2:12). The son of David, the Messiah, the Lord—sharing a crib with farm animals! But this really was a message of glory, for the cloud-like scene becomes more awesome still: "Suddenly a great company of the heavenly host appeared with the angel, praising God and saying, 'Glory to God in the highest heaven, and on earth peace to those on whom his favor rests" (Luke 2:13–14). What a striking contrast: the angelic throng proclaims God's glory above for a child born in a stall below.

When Jesus begins his earthly ministry, the theme of glory-cloaked-in-humility continues. In his first miracle recorded in John, Jesus joins a common human celebration, a wedding, and turns water into wine—but does so behind the scenes, invisible to the eye and known only to servants (John 2:1–9). A miracle with no outward adornment, yet John declares: "What Jesus did here in Cana of Galilee was the first of the signs through which he revealed his glory" (John 2:11).

---

6.   This translation is my own.
7.   Theologians often distinguish between Christ's states of "humiliation" and "exaltation," the former referring to the period between his incarnation and death/burial, and the latter consisting in his resurrection, ascension, and continuing reign at God's right hand. E.g., see Louis Berkhof, *Systematic Theology* (Grand Rapids: Eerdmans, 1993), 331–54.

The glory-in-humility paradox stands out still more distinctly in the account of Jesus' transfiguration, which casts our eyes back to the Old Testament pillar of cloud and fire and ahead to Christ's heavenly glory on the last day. As Jesus was praying, "the appearance of his face changed, and his clothes became as bright as a flash of lightning. Two men, Moses and Elijah, appeared in glorious splendor, talking with Jesus" (Luke 9:29–30). His disciples "saw his glory" and, when Peter offered to build three shelters for them, "a cloud appeared and covered them" (Luke 9:34). Many years later, Peter recounted this event: "We were eyewitnesses of his majesty. He received honor and glory from God the Father when the voice came to him from the Majestic Glory" (2 Pet 1:16–17). Yet Luke surrounds his description of Jesus' glory in the transfiguration with many reminders of his call to suffer, and of his followers' call to suffer with him. Immediately prior to the account of the transfiguration, Jesus told his disciples: "The Son of Man must suffer many things and be rejected by the elders, the chief priests and the teachers of the law, and he must be killed and on the third day be raised to life," then he added: "Whoever wants to be my disciple must deny [himself] and take up [his] cross daily and follow me" (Luke 9:22–23). Following the transfiguration story, Jesus states, "the Son of Man is going to be delivered into the hands of men" (Luke 9:44), and he explains the cost of following him (Luke 9:57–62).

The glory-in-humility dynamic also emerges in the raising of Lazarus, perhaps the most dramatic and astounding of Jesus' miracles. When Jesus first heard of Lazarus' illness, he assured his disciples. "This sickness will not end in death. No, it is for God's glory so that God's Son may be glorified through it" (John 11:4). But this glorification, he explains later to Martha, would only take place *through death*: "I am the resurrection and the life. The one who believes in me will live, even though [he] die[s]" (John 11:25). Later he tells Martha, "if you believe, you will see the glory of God" (John 11:40), and then he calls Lazarus from the tomb. But even then it results not in an earthly triumph for Christ, but prompts the chief priests and the Pharisees to call a meeting of the Sanhedrin to plot his arrest (John 11:45–57).

Evident in many of the texts just considered is that glory belongs both to Christ and to God the Father. Earlier we saw an intimate relationship between Son and Spirit, and we see the same thing between Father and Son. This theme pervades all four gospels but is especially prominent in John. Jesus is glorified in so many of his works—such as turning water into wine, the transfiguration, and the raising of Lazarus—yet he did not come to glorify himself. Instead, the Father glorifies him: "I am not seeking glory for myself; but there is one who seeks it, and he is the judge" (John 8:50). "If I glorify myself, my glory means nothing. My Father . . . is the one who glorifies me" (John 8:54). As the Epistle to the Hebrews echoes, "Christ did not take on himself the glory of becoming a high priest," but was appointed by God (Heb 5:4–6).

Not only did the Father glorify the Son, but the Son also glorified the Father, and this especially through his obedience. "I have brought you glory on earth," Jesus prayed, "by finishing the work you gave me to do" (John 17:4). Jesus presents quite a contrast to the disobedient Israelites, who would not obey God's will and hence were repelled by God's glory rather than exalted by it. While John slows the action and builds dramatic tension as his gospel reaches the final week of Jesus' life, he makes increasingly explicit how the Father and Son mutually glorify each other. After the triumphal entry, Jesus prophesies his death and prays: "'Father, glorify your name!' Then a voice came from heaven, 'I have glorified it, and will glorify it again'" (John 12:28). During the Last Supper Jesus declares, "Now the Son of Man is glorified and God is glorified in him. If God is glorified in him, God will glorify the Son in himself, and will glorify him at once" (John 13:31–32). The same theme saturates Christ's beloved "high priestly prayer," which begins, "Father, the hour has come. Glorify your Son, that your Son may glorify you" (John 17:1). Shortly thereafter, he prays: "I have brought you glory on earth by finishing the work you gave me to do. And now, Father, glorify me in your presence with the glory I had with you before the world began" (John 17:4–5).

In this amazing Trinitarian dynamic chronicled in John's gospel—the Spirit empowers the Son to do glorious works, the Son glorifies the Father in his obedience to the Father's will, and the Father in turn glorifies his obedient Son—it is remarkable how the story of God's glory that began in the Old Testament converges upon Calvary. The drama of God's glory meeting human sinners comes to this: one who is both God's eternal glory and a true man bearing the curse of sin is lifted up—on a cross. Although in one sense Christ's earthly ministry is about suffering and his exaltation is about glory, in another sense the Trinitarian God is glorified *through* Christ's crucifixion (and not simply *after* it). When Jesus says, "The hour has come for the Son of Man to be glorified," he goes on to explain that a kernel of wheat must fall to the ground and die if it is to produce many seeds (John 12:23–24). He continues, "Now my soul is troubled, and what shall I say? 'Father, save me from this hour'? No, it was for this very reason

I came to this hour. Father, glorify your name!" (John 12:27–28). In other words, in regard to the approach of his death—at which he confesses to being troubled—Jesus glorifies the name of his Father. A few days later, on the night he is betrayed, following Judas' departure, Jesus says, "*Now* the Son of Man is glorified and God is glorified in him" (John 13:31). Likewise, he begins his High Priestly prayer: "Father, *the hour* has come. Glorify your Son, that your Son may glorify you. . . . I have brought you glory on earth *by finishing the work* you gave me to do" (John 17:1, 4). "Jesus' glory," indeed, "is particularly revealed in the cross."[8]

The climactic work of Christ at Calvary was the ultimate in humiliation, shame, and reproach. Yet the Father gave him this work to do, Christ did it by the Spirit, and the persons of the Holy Trinity glorified themselves through it. The immeasurable love of God is on full display, for Christ's obedience unto death—"even death on a cross" (Phil 2:8)—was precisely what we sinners needed for salvation. We observed earlier how God wills to be glorified through his works in this world and even in and through us. Here the Lord displays this in stark beauty: God wills to be glorified precisely through reconciling us to himself, and he does so through the cross (cf. Rom 5:10; 2 Cor 5:18–21; Col 1:21–22).

The Glory of Christ in His Exaltation

Christ's humble life and brutal death brought glory to him and his Father, though a glory invisible to human eyes. But the dark night of Calvary gave way to the bright dawn of the resurrection, and Christ's humiliation to his exaltation. With his resurrection and subsequent ascension to the right hand of the Father, the glory of the Son of God is no longer veiled. What was for a time shrouded in earthly disgrace and gore now illumines the heavenly kingdom.

During Jesus' earthly ministry, his disciples apparently had some sense of the glory their Lord would someday enjoy. James and John, for example, could make the audacious request: "Let one of us sit at your right and the other at your left in your glory" (Mark 10:37). In light of this attitude, Jesus was less concerned about his glory to come and much more concerned to instruct his disciples about his imminent sufferings—he responds to James and John by speaking of the cup of wrath he must drink (Mark 10:39; cf. Isa 51:17) and the ransom price he must pay (Mark 10:45).

---

8. Thomas R. Schreiner, *New Testament Theology: Magnifying God in Christ* (Grand Rapids: Baker Academic, 2008), 243; cf. 284.

While the disciples, prior to Calvary, never seemed fully to grasp what Jesus had to undergo, after the cross the weight of his sufferings so crushed their spirits that their previous dreams of his future glory apparently vanished. When Jesus, unrecognized, met two of them on the road to Emmaus on resurrection Sunday, they recounted the women's report, their vision of angels, and the empty tomb—but seemed to have no idea what to make of it (Luke 24:13–24). Jesus said to them, "'How foolish you are, and how slow to believe all that the prophets have spoken! Did not the Messiah have to suffer these things and then enter his glory?' And beginning with Moses and all the Prophets, he explained to them what was said in all the Scriptures concerning himself" (Luke 24:25–27). Only after they had seen Jesus crucified and resurrected could the disciples finally begin to grasp how the story of Christ's humiliation-then-glorification fit together, how it was prophesied in the Old Testament, and how it is the centerpiece of salvation. Concerning Jesus' triumphal entry into Jerusalem, a picture of both Jesus' lowliness and majesty, John writes: "At first his disciples did not understand all this. Only after Jesus was glorified did they realize that these things had been written about him and that these things had been done to him" (John 12:16; cf. Ps 118:25–26; Zech 9:9).

But once Jesus' disciples grasped the divine plan, it became the theme of their missionary preaching. In Peter's first sermon after the Day of Pentecost, he proclaimed: "The God of Abraham, Isaac and Jacob, the God of our fathers, has glorified his servant Jesus. . . . You killed the author of life, but God raised him from the dead. We are witnesses of this" (Acts 3:13, 15). Years later Peter reflects on the Old Testament prophecies whose meaning so baffled them during Jesus' earthly life, but in which he now sees the great gospel story of humiliation-then-glory. The Old Testament prophets "searched intently and with the greatest care, trying to find out the time and circumstances to which the Spirit of Christ in them was pointing when he predicted the sufferings of the Messiah and the glories that would follow" (1 Pet 1:10–11). Continuing this same theme a few verses later, Peter speaks of our redemption by "the precious blood of Christ, a lamb without blemish or defect," through whom his readers had believed in God, "who raised him from the dead and glorified him" (1 Pet 1:18–19, 21). Similarly, Paul explains that Christ "was raised from the dead through the glory of the Father" (Rom 6:4) and now has a "body of glory" (Phil 3:21).[9]

---

9.   This is my translation of Philippians 3:21.

When Paul spoke of Christ being raised by the glory of the Father and with a body of glory, he likely had the Holy Spirit on his mind. Elsewhere he writes of "the Spirit of him who raised Jesus from the dead" (Rom 8:11) and describes Jesus' resurrected body as a "spiritual" (or, even better, a "Spiritual") body (1 Cor 15:44). Peter also ascribed a special role to the Spirit in Jesus' resurrection to glory: Christ "was put to death in the body but made alive in the Spirit" (1 Pet 3:18; cf. 1 Tim 3:16).

Thus Jesus' resurrection is vital to the larger story of divine glory we've been tracing over the past two chapters. The Old Testament portrayed the glorious pillar of cloud as a visible manifestation of the Holy Spirit leading and instructing the Israelites. In the New Testament, the Spirit was God's instrument of the Son's incarnation. He visibly descended upon Christ in his baptism, empowered him in his ministry, and even led him to the cross. Then the Spirit of glory raised Jesus from the dead, clothing him with a body that is at once "glorious" and "Spiritual" (Phil 3:21; 1 Cor 15:44).

Even the resurrection, however, does not bring this story of divine glory to its close. After being raised in glory, Christ "was taken up in glory" (1 Tim 3:16). The one who "was made lower than the angels for a little while" is "now crowned with glory and honor" (Heb 2:9). This refers to his reign in "the world to come," which God designed the human race to rule (Heb 2:5–8). Hebrews 2:5–9 is amazing to contemplate. From the beginning God wanted human beings, not angels, to rule the world to come, but now we don't see evidence of it. Yet "we do see Jesus," who became like us in our humility and is now exalted in glory. In Jesus' human flesh and blood the original destiny of the human race finds its fulfillment. As we'll marvel at in the next chapter, this exalted Jesus is also now "bringing many sons to glory" (Heb 2:10)—that is, he'll lead his people to fill the new creation with glorified human beings, with bodies raised like his. And while we wait for this final day, we have a delightful foretaste of the full banquet ahead. When Christ received the Spirit as a victory gift from his Father upon ascending to heaven, he in turn "poured [him] out" upon his people on the Day of Pentecost (Acts 2:33). That Spirit is now the seal and guarantee of our share in the glorious feast to come (see 2 Cor 1:22; 5:5; Eph 1:13–14; 4:30).

The Glory of the Heavenly Kingdom

The glory of God revealed in the pillar of cloud and fire was magnificent, but never fully satisfactory. The cloud appeared and disappeared. It came to rest, then moved again. It drew near to the people in blessing but then judged them for disobedience. Even Moses, who stood in its midst, longed for greater intimacy with God. The Old Testament cloud simultaneously revealed God's glory to Israel and kept the people at a distance. But the Old Testament also pointed to a day when God's glory would return to the Israelites after the disgrace of exile and bring abounding and unshakable blessing not only to them but also to the Gentiles. A new and better temple would arise upon which the glory of God would never cease to rest.

What the rebuilt temple in Jerusalem could never hope to fulfill is finally achieved in the heavenly city, the New Jerusalem, at whose center Christ sits enthroned. The earthly sanctuary where the Levitical priests ministered was only "a copy of the true one" (Heb 9:24); its sacrifices were "not the realities themselves" (Heb 10:1). The blood of goats and bulls offered there could never truly take away sin and thus enable the worshipers to commune with the living God in their midst (Heb 10:4). But Christ, through suffering, has become a perfect and effective high priest for his people (Heb 5:7–10) and has purified them once and for all (Heb 10:10–18). He achieved for them fellowship with God not merely in an earthly sanctuary but in one not made with human hands (Heb 9:11), a heavenly sanctuary into which a "new and living way" has been opened for us that we might "draw near to God with a sincere heart and with full assurance" (Heb 10:19–22). At present, we have not yet entered that sanctuary with resurrected bodies, but as sojourning Abraham of old, we long "for a better country—a heavenly one," for the "enduring city . . . that is to come" (Heb 11:16; 13:14). There, "exalted above the heavens," is a high priest who "truly meets our need" and "always lives to intercede" for us (Heb 7: 26). The cloud of old drew near to the people, but could not ultimately welcome them into divine fellowship even in an earthly sanctuary. Now the heavenly sanctuary has welcomed the Lord Jesus Christ in our own flesh and blood.

And through him what great glory fills the sanctuary in that enduring city, which the glory of the old sanctuary in the earthly Jerusalem just faintly reflected. Stephen, the first Christian martyr, had the privilege of catching a glimpse of what all believers will one day behold: he "looked up to heaven and saw the glory of God, and Jesus standing at the right hand of God" (Acts 7:55). Even this can hardly compare with John's visions of heavenly glory throughout the book of Revelation. John is taken up "in the Spirit," and that means he stood before the throne of heaven (Rev 4:2). Before the brilliant majesty of the one who sits upon that throne (Rev 4:3), the living creatures and the twenty-four elders ascribe glory and honor

(Rev 4:9, 11). John sees a lamb "standing at the center of the throne," a Lamb who had been slain (Rev 5:6). "Thousands upon thousands, and ten thousand times ten thousand" angels encircle the throne and cry out: "Worthy is the Lamb, who was slain, to receive power and wealth and wisdom and strength and honor and glory and praise" (Rev 5:11–12). For anyone counting, that is one hundred million angels declaring the once crucified Christ worthy of all glory. Their song echoes and echoes in the pages that follow (Rev 7:12; 15:4; 19:1). Here is the glory of the new and better temple which we heard the Old Testament prophets proclaiming to beleaguered exiles, and which should still gladden the hearts of Christians today, exiles in the world but citizens of heaven (Phil 3:20; 1 Pet 2:11).

Christ is now exalted in heaven, but even this does not complete the biblical story of divine glory. The story reaches its climax only with Christ's second coming. How fascinating, in light of the course of the story in the Old Testament, that Christ is going to come again in a glorious *cloud*. The peoples of the world, says Jesus, will "see the Son of Man coming on the clouds with power and great glory" (Matt 24:30). Elsewhere Jesus describes it a little differently—"the Son of Man is going to come in his Father's glory with his angels" (Matt 16:27; cf. Mark 8:38; Luke 9:26)—but by now we recognize that these various images point to the same great reality: the visible, majestic, and awesome presence of God.

How does the story of divine glory climax in Christ's second coming? In part, it climaxes through Christ judging and conquering his enemies. As the cloud of glory descended upon Israel of old, so will this cloud descend upon the whole world at the last day, accompanying the Lord Jesus Christ to execute a judgment far greater than what Israel endured—a final judgment. Scripture uses various means to describe God's glory in judging his enemies. Ezekiel speaks of a final battle between God and the enemy nations, symbolized as "Gog, of the land of Magog" (Ezek 38–39). In this decisive defeat of Gog, the Lord says, "I will display my glory among the nations, and all the nations see the punishment I inflict and the hand I lay on them" (Ezek 39:21). Revelation also speaks of God's final triumph over his enemies, but here especially through the image of "Babylon." Immediately before announcing, "Fallen! Fallen is Babylon the Great, which made all the nations drink the maddening wine of her adulteries" (Rev 14:8), an angel proclaims "in a loud voice, 'Fear God and give him glory, because the hour of his judgment has come'" (Rev 14:7). Jesus described the final judgment in the following way: "When the Son of Man comes in his glory, and all the angels with him, he will sit on his glorious throne," and "all the nations will be gathered before him, and he will separate the people one from another as a shepherd separates the sheep from the goats" (Matt 25:31–32; cf. 19:28).[10]

The final victory Christ wins over his enemies is a sobering topic that even many Christians find unpalatable. It is important to remember that those conquered on the last day are *enemies* of God. They have opposed God, rejected his truth, and often persecuted his people. Their persecution of Christians is also why God's final judgment of his enemies is part of the good news of salvation for us. This decisive conquest of the gospel's enemies will bring relief to suffering believers and deliverance from every snare and temptation. Paul reminds the Thessalonians, for example, of the "everlasting destruction" coming upon the wicked at the revelation of the Lord Jesus "from heaven in blazing fire with his powerful angels" (more imagery of the cloud of divine glory). He explains, "God is just: he will pay back trouble to those who trouble you and give relief to you who are troubled, and to us as well" (2 Thess 1:6–7).

Christian believers, however, may look forward to that amazing day not simply because God will judge their enemies for their benefit. Immediately following the words from 2 Thessalonians quoted above, Paul adds a positive dimension: on that great day Christ "comes to be glorified in his holy people and to be marveled at among all those who have believed" (2 Thess 1:10). This is astounding. Jesus will not only glorify himself at his second coming by donning the pillar of cloud and fire as a cloak and leading the throng of heavenly angels in his train, but he will also glorify himself *in his saints.* No wonder our "blessed hope" is "the appearing of the glory of our great God and Savior, Jesus Christ" (Titus 2:13).

Although fierce temptations and seemingly unbearable persecutions weigh Christians down, Peter encourages us to "rejoice inasmuch as you participate in the sufferings of Christ, so that you may be overjoyed when his glory is revealed" (1 Pet 4:13). On that day we will see "a new heaven and a new earth," and the "Holy City, the new Jerusalem, coming down out of heaven from God" (Rev 21:1–2). It will shine "with the glory of God, and its brilliance [will be] like that of a very precious jewel, like a

---

10. On a related note, Jonathan Edwards writes: "This [God's glory] is spoken of as the end [i.e., the goal] of the execution of God's threatenings in the punishment of sin. . . ." (Num 14:20–23). "This is spoken of as the end of God executing judgments on his enemies in this world" (Exod 14:17–18; Ezek 28:22; 39:13). "And this is spoken of as the end, both of the executions of wrath and in the glorious exercises of mercy, in the misery and happiness of another world" (see Rom 9:22–23; 2 Thess 1:9–10). Edwards, "The End for Which God Created the World," in John Piper, *God's Passion for His Glory*, 208–09.

jasper, clear as crystal" (Rev 21:11). We, too, at last will be welcomed into the glory of the greater sanctuary where Christ has been ministering on our behalf since his ascension. Revelation 21 also corrects a possible misunderstanding. When Hebrews speaks about Christ ministering in a heavenly sanctuary (Heb 9), it does not teach that there is a separate temple within the heavenly city. To be precise, the city has no temple, "because the Lord God Almighty and the Lamb are its temple" (Rev 21:22). Jesus, the Immanuel—God with us—will be there with us face to face, so no other temple is necessary. And neither does the city "need the sun or the moon to shine on it, for the glory of God gives it light, and the Lamb is its lamp" (Rev 21:23). How fitting. When we dwell in the midst of a pillar of fire capable of illuminating the desert of Sinai in the dark of night, and the light of the world sits enthroned at city center, the starry host becomes wholly superfluous.

Christ, the Brightness of His Father's Glory

We began this chapter on a disheartening note. The approach of God's glory to his Old Testament people in the pillar of cloud and fire never turned out well. The story seemed to come to an insuperable barrier when the cloud departed from the temple in Jerusalem and God exiled the Israelites to Babylon. But God promised something new and something much better. The Old Testament prophets foresaw that glory would return in a new temple, an indestructible temple to which all the nations would come. The New Testament apostles announce the fulfillment of all these promises—through Christ, in whom all God's promises are Yes, so that in Christ "the 'Amen' is spoken by us to the glory of God" (2 Cor 1:20). He is the brightness of his Father's glory, the one who brought him glory in the disgrace of the cross and through his ascension to the Father's right hand in the majesty of heaven. He will also bring him glory when he returns on a cloud with the angelic host.

The last great truths we considered in this chapter take us to matters of primary concern in the next chapter. We really are not able to bring this biblical story of God's glory to completion without understanding our place in the plot. Glory belongs to God alone—*soli Deo gloria*—but he is pleased to bring all glory to himself in part by glorifying us in Christ. To this great theme we now turn.

CHAPTER 5

The Glory of Christ in the Glorification of His People

"We all, who with unveiled faces contemplate the Lord's glory, are being transformed into his image with ever-increasing glory, which comes from the Lord, who is the Spirit." —*2 Corinthians 3:18*

"Therefore we do not lose heart. Though outwardly we are wasting away, yet inwardly we are being renewed day by day. For our light and momentary troubles are achieving for us an eternal glory that far outweighs them all." —*2 Corinthians 4:16–17*

All glory belongs to God. The Reformation affirmed this because Scripture could hardly say it more clearly. But Scripture also teaches that Christians are glorified—they somehow participate in the glory of God in Christ. It is not immediately clear how both can be true. How can *all* glory belong to God while human creatures simultaneously share in his glory?

To some degree, the answer to this question is a mystery that defies purely rational explanation. The God of all glory glorifies his creatures, and sinful creatures at that—surely this should prompt wonder and gratitude more than intellectual analysis. Yet the story of divine glory traced in the previous two chapters does provide a theological framework to help us understand why there is no ultimate contradiction in the twin biblical truths that all glory belongs to God and that Christians are glorified in Christ.

Although God is internally glorious, he wills to reveal his glory in and through the world he's made. He does so through the beauty of the natural order as a whole, but also, and especially, through drawing near to his chosen people and manifesting a greater vision of divine glory to them. In the Old Testament, the pillar of cloud and fire overshadowed the Israelites in the wilderness and eventually rested upon their temple in Jerusalem. That presence of divine glory, however, could not abide the people's wretched sin, and so the cloud departed from the temple, and God drove them into exile. But in the fullness of time, God sent forth his Son, the brightness of his Father's glory, as the true and enduring temple, the Immanuel—God with us. He veiled his glory through days of humiliation, all for the sake of poor sinners, to deliver his people from the guilt and pollution that made them unworthy to commune with the presence of God in their midst. But God also raised his Son from the grave and exalted him to the throne in his heavenly kingdom, of which the cloud of old was only a faint replica. A man of our own flesh and blood sits enthroned in the glory of his Father. And he will not be satisfied until a multitude of his brothers and sisters join him in that everlasting city, their very bodies being glorified with his, proclaiming his praise in unceasing beatitude.

The glorification of believers in Christ *is* the glorification of God. To confess *soli Deo gloria* is to proclaim, in part, that he *alone* has worked such a great salvation—by grace, through faith, in Christ. Christians will not share Christ's glory in the sense that anyone will ever bow down and worship them, but in the supreme glorification of Christ, believers are swept up into abiding communion with their Lord. Their holiness, their righteousness, and even their bodies will reflect the glory of their king. The glorification of his people redounds to the glory of God.

The theme of Christians' glorification now becomes our focus. In this chapter we consider how Scripture unpacks the glorification of believers for the glory of God. As with our Lord, this glorification comes by the Spirit, and only through the way of suffering. In light of these ideas, we can appreciate our calling to glorify God in our worship, now and indeed throughout our entire lives.

Glorification: Human Destiny Achieved

Understanding humanity's glorification requires turning our thoughts back to creation. Although it is only through salvation in Christ that we can now attain that ultimate destiny of blessed life in the new Jerusalem, it is helpful to recognize that even before the fall into sin (and hence before the need for salvation) God created human beings to reflect his glory.

The terminology of "glory" doesn't appear in Genesis 1, but the fact that God created humans in his *image* conveys this idea. The notions of image and glory are closely conjoined later in Scripture. Paul says that man is "the image and glory of God" (1 Cor 11:7) and speaks of "the glory of Christ, who is the image of God" (2 Cor 4:4). Christ is both "the radiance of God's glory and the exact representation of his being" (Heb 1:3), and Christians "are being transformed into his image with ever-increasing glory" (2 Cor 3:18). Thus, to say that God created humans in his image in Genesis 1:26 implies that they reflected the glory of God.[1]

This impression is strengthened by the fact that Genesis 1 itself probably speaks about the cloud of divine glory. Genesis 1:2 says that "the earth was formless and empty, darkness was over the surface of the deep, and the Spirit of God was hovering over the waters." This is likely telling us that the cloud in the wilderness first appeared here, overshadowing the earth after God called it into existence.[2] Genesis 1:2 says that the *Spirit* hovered over the waters, and, as considered in earlier chapters, Scripture often speaks of the cloud as a manifestation of the Spirit. Furthermore, although it is difficult to appreciate fully by looking only at an English translation, in the original Hebrew, the vocabulary of two verses in the song of Moses that describe the pillar of cloud and fire over Israel in the wilderness is strikingly similar to the vocabulary of Genesis 1:2: "In a desert land he found him, in a barren and howling waste. He shielded him and cared for him . . . , like an eagle that stirs up its nest and hovers over its young" (Deut 32:10–11). The shared vocabulary is surely not accidental; the Spirit hovering over the original void and the cloud hovering over the wilderness waste were one and the same. The language of Genesis 1:26 confirms this conclusion. Here God speaks in the plural: "Let *us* make mankind in our image." This is the language of God's heavenly court; how he speaks when surrounded by his angelic host (see Isa 6:8). And as considered above, angels often adorn the cloud of glory.[3]

Genesis 1 thus strongly suggests that God made human beings as creatures reflecting his glory, as images of the God who spoke out of the pillar of cloud and fire by his Spirit. Scripture later looks back at creation and speaks of this more explicitly. Psalm 8, for example, begins by extolling God's own glory: "LORD, our Lord, how majestic is your name in all the

---

1. For further discussion of the image of God and glory of God, see also Meredith G. Kline, *Images of the Spirit* (Grand Rapids: Baker, 1980), chap. 1.

2. See Chapter 3 for additional discussion and references related to this idea.

3. For a more detailed defense of this heavenly court view of Genesis 1:26, see David VanDrunen, *Divine Covenants and Moral Order: A Biblical Theology of Natural Law* (Grand Rapids: Eerdmans, 2014), 538–42.

earth! You have set your glory in the heavens" (Ps 8:1). But it quickly moves on to reflect on the privileges God bestowed on human beings: "You have made them a little lower than the angels and crowned them with glory and honor. You made them rulers over the works of your hands; you put everything under their feet" (Ps 8:5–6). A similar theme appears in Psalm 115. "Not to us, LORD, not to us," it opens, "but to your name be the glory" (Ps 115:1). Later, it adds: "The highest heavens belong to the LORD, but the earth he has given to mankind. . . . It is we who extol the LORD, both now and forevermore" (Ps 115:16–17). All glory was God's in the original creation, but he created human beings in his image to have dominion over the other creatures. God crowned us with honor and glory—yet all glory belongs to God and not to us. This beautiful tension was already present at creation.

But what a mess we made of it. When the epistle to the Hebrews speaks of how God honored human beings by commissioning them to rule, the author fittingly quotes Psalm 8:4–6 (Heb 2:5–7). Then, with almost humorous understatement, he wryly comments: "Yet at present we do not see everything subject to him" (Heb 2:8). That's for sure. There are many ways we can characterize the first sin in the Garden of Eden, but many theologians have highlighted the *pride* of Adam and Eve, and at the heart of pride is a desire for self-glory. God made them in his image—an astounding blessing and a position of true honor—but lured by the serpent, they longed to "be like God" in their own way rather than under God's rightful authority. Rather than ruling over the other creatures in submission to God, they let themselves be ruled by a creature and tried to submit God to themselves.

Self-glorification has become the hallmark of sinful humanity in the footsteps of its father Adam. The great city of Babylon was legendary for its pride: "You said in your heart, 'I will ascend to the heavens; I will raise my throne above the stars of God; I will sit enthroned on the mount of assembly, on the utmost heights of Mount Zaphon. I will ascend above the tops of the clouds; I will make myself like the Most High'" (Isa 14:13–14). Babylon later becomes symbolic of rebellious humanity in general, as the great world-city that God will overthrow on the last day. She gives herself "glory and luxury," and "In her heart she boasts, 'I sit enthroned as queen'" (Rev 18:7). Ironically, this prideful self-glorification is actually degrading. When sinful humans "knew God" but "neither glorified him as God nor gave thanks to him," they "exchanged the glory of the immortal God for images made to look like a mortal human being and birds and animals and reptiles" (Rom 1:21, 23). They "exchanged the truth about God for a lie, and worshiped and served created things rather than the Creator" (Rom 1:25). We see such an important truth here. God made us in his image to reflect his glory, but obliged us to bow before his supreme authority. As soon as we tried to usurp his honor and, dissatisfied with the great privileges he granted, sought to glorify ourselves, we became mired in miserable idolatry, unable to rule the world or to rescue ourselves. With truth, the author of Hebrews remarks that we don't now see the glory and honor of human beings ruling under the authority of the all-glorious God.

But, he also says, "we do see Jesus" (Heb 2:9). In Jesus the glory of humanity is realized, and through him a redeemed host of fellow human beings will declare God's praise in the heavenly assembly (Heb 2:10–13). But before reflecting further on this, I need to emphasize that the attainment of glory in Christ was not a brand-new idea of God's but the realization of his original design, which he would not allow the forces of evil to thwart. The argument in Hebrews 2 we've been considering begins with the statement, "It is not to angels that he [God] has subjected the world to come" (Heb 2:5). The author proves this by quoting Psalm 8, which speaks of God's gift of dominion to human beings at creation. The implication is that God created human beings to rule from the beginning, even before the fall, and destined them to rule not only this present creation but also the new creation, the "world to come." By sending Jesus, who is "now crowned with glory and honor" and "bringing many sons . . . to glory" in his train (Heb 2:9–10), God is thereby accomplishing what he originally designed: human beings as faithful image-bearers who rule under God in the glory of the heavenly kingdom. Adam's fall meant that God would bring this about through a different means, but the ultimate end remained the same. And it is not as if the fall caught God by surprise and left him scrambling to construct Plan B. Rather, the "mystery" of salvation through the cross of Christ, though long "hidden" from human imagination, was "destined [by God] for our glory before time began" (1 Cor 2:7).

Thus, the story of divine glory runs not only through Calvary but also through Christ's transformation of sinners through his Holy Spirit. Perhaps no biblical statement sums this up so beautifully as 2 Corinthians 3:18: "We all, who with unveiled faces contemplate the Lord's glory, are being transformed into his image with ever-increasing glory, which comes from the Lord, who is the Spirit." This wonderful reality, beginning even now and awaiting completion in the age to come, is indeed a gift of Christ.

He said to his Father on the night he was betrayed, "I have given them the glory that you gave me" (John 17:22).

When we speak of "the gospel," we often think of the basic good news of forgiveness of sins through Jesus Christ. This is not inaccurate, but it is helpful to remember that the gospel message is ultimately about God's own glory and includes all the benefits of salvation, including the goal of God's grace: our glorification with Christ in the new creation. Paul speaks of "the gospel concerning the glory of the blessed God, which he entrusted to me" (1 Tim 1:11), and this gospel of God's glory entails our glorification: "He called you to this through our gospel, that you might share in the glory of our Lord Jesus Christ" (2 Thess 2:14). This expectation of glory was apparently at the center of Paul's preaching: "God has chosen to make known among the Gentiles the glorious riches of this mystery, which is Christ in you, the hope of glory. He is the one we proclaim" (Col 1:27–28). Or as he puts it elsewhere: "What we preach is not ourselves, but Jesus Christ as Lord. . . . For God, who said, 'Let light shine out of darkness,' made his light shine in our hearts to give us the light of the knowledge of God's glory displayed in the face of Christ" (2 Cor 4:5–6). The glory of God, the glory of Christ, the glorification of believers—all, it seems, are part of one grand gospel message.

The Spirit, Suffering, and the Glory to Come

God's glorification of himself through the glorification of believers in Christ has many aspects. Before we examine a few of them specifically it may be helpful to keep in mind that our theological term, "glorification," refers to future blessings.[4] With death, Christians attain some of these blessings, especially liberation from their sinful natures. Then, at Christ's return, they will gain the full blessings of glorification. God will raise their bodies and grant them complete enjoyment of the new creation. While we continue our earthly pilgrimage, however, God grants many foretastes of what's to come. Through justification and adoption, he already grants us citizenship and an inheritance in the new Jerusalem, and through sanctification he already begins to put to death our sinful natures. In light of this, we can understand why the New Testament primarily speaks about our glorification as something yet to be attained, yet also sometimes uses this language to describe our present Christian experience.

---

4. E.g., see the treatment of glorification in John Murray, *Redemption: Accomplished and Applied* (Grand Rapids: Eerdmans, 1955), 217–24.

We will now consider three aspects of our participation in Christ's glory: the role of the Holy Spirit, the call to suffer here and now, and our glorification on the last day. In all three we observe the pattern of Christ's experience reflected in our own. As Christ on his path to glory was led by the Spirit, through the way of the cross, to the triumph of the new creation, so it is for Christians being re-created in his image.

First, then, our participation in the glory of Christ comes only through the blessing of the Holy Spirit. Previous chapters have considered the centrality of the Spirit for the revelation of God's glory. The Old Testament associated the cloud of glory with the Spirit leading Israel through the wilderness and prophesied that the Spirit would clothe the coming Messiah. The Spirit then worked the Son's incarnation in Mary's womb and empowered him through his earthly ministry. By the Spirit, God raised him from the dead with a "glorious" and "Spiritual" body (Phil 3:21; 1 Cor 15:44). If we are to enjoy some share in the glory of Christ, then we would expect to share in the blessing and power of the Spirit.

Although there is plenty of evidence that the Spirit was at work in believers in important ways before Christ's coming, the Old Testament also points to a richer outpouring of the Spirit in the Messianic days after Israel's exile. For example, Ezekiel declares: "I will give you a new heart and put a new spirit in you; I will remove from you your heart of stone and give you a heart of flesh. And I will put my Spirit in you and move you to follow my decrees and be careful to keep my laws" (Ezek 36:26–27). As Jesus was carrying out his earthly ministry, he made a cryptic statement that signals the fulfillment of this promise: "Let anyone who is thirsty come to me and drink. Whoever believes in me, as Scripture has said, rivers of living water will flow from within [him]" (literally, "from his belly") (John 7:37–38). At this point in the text, John interrupts his narrative and offers a brief explanation: "By this he meant the Spirit, whom those who believed in him were later to receive. Up to that time the Spirit had not been given, since Jesus had not yet been glorified" (John 7:39).

So here we have it. Only with Jesus' glorification—that is, his exaltation to heaven—would we come to enjoy this greater gift of the Spirit. The Spirit of glory was not Jesus' to share until he finished his work and attained, in our flesh, the exalted glory to which the Spirit led him. This pouring forth of the Spirit at Christ's exaltation, furthermore, would serve to glorify Christ. As Jesus told his disciples later in the gospel of John: "When he, the Spirit of truth, comes, he will guide you into all the truth. He will not speak on his own; he will speak only what he hears. . . . He will glorify me because it is from me that he will receive what he will make known to you" (John 16:13–14).

On the day of Pentecost, when miniature pillars of fire rested upon each disciple (and not merely upon the community as a whole, as with the Israelites in the wilderness), Peter explained what was going on to the puzzled crowd: "God has raised this Jesus to life, and we are all witnesses of it. Exalted to the right hand of God, he has received from the Father the promised Holy Spirit and has poured out what you now see and hear" (Acts 2:32–33). Following his ascension, therefore, Christ gives to us the Spirit given to him at his glorification—so that Christ's glory may begin to be revealed in us, too. In case there is any doubt that Christ intended this gift for *all* believers and not simply the apostles, Peter later explained, speaking to the church generally, "the Spirit of glory and of God rests on you" (1 Pet 4:14).

Paul also emphasized how the completion of Christ's work meant the pouring forth of the Spirit, and hence also a greater glory than Israel of old experienced. In 2 Corinthians 3, he reflects on a fact we observed in Chapters 3–4, namely, that the revelation of God's glory to Israel, magnificent as it was, ended up bringing the people into judgment, since their sin made them unworthy to abide in God's presence.

> Now if the ministry that brought death, which was engraved in letters on stone, came with glory . . . , will not the ministry of the Spirit be even more glorious? If the ministry that brought condemnation was glorious, how much more glorious is the ministry that brings righteousness! For what was glorious has no glory now in comparison with the surpassing glory. And if what was transitory came with glory, how much greater is the glory of that which lasts (2 Cor 3:7–11)!

What a wonderful truth that with the new covenant—sealed by Christ's death, his resurrection, and the pouring forth of the Spirit—the condemnation of sin no longer makes us unfit to participate in the glory of God. Hence Paul concludes 2 Corinthians 3 with these words: "Now the Lord is the Spirit, and where the Spirit of the Lord is, there is freedom. And we all, who with unveiled faces contemplate the Lord's glory, are being transformed into his image with ever-increasing glory, which comes from the Lord, who is the Spirit" (3:17–18).

An important way in which Scripture describes the ministry of the Holy Spirit is that the Spirit unites us to Christ (e.g., 1 Cor 12:12–13). The members of the church are knit together as a single body, joined to Christ their head (1 Cor 12:12–27); he is the vine, we are the branches

(John 15:1–11); we are a holy structure built on Christ the foundation and cornerstone (Eph 2:18–22; 1 Cor 3:11). The nearness of God in the pillar of cloud and fire under the old covenant was only a mixed blessing. But under the new covenant, the nearness of Christ through his Spirit joins us in a most intimate and unbreakable fellowship.

Here, then, is the first important theme that communicates how Christians share in Christ's glory. The glory that rested over the tabernacle now rests upon each one of us, making us temples of the Holy Spirit (1 Cor 6:19). The Spirit, who revealed God's glory in the cloud of old and now most eminently in Christ enthroned in heaven, is already at work in us. To have Christ's Spirit is to have a share in Christ's glory.

Second, our participation in Christ's glory not only comes by the Spirit but also through the way of suffering. The gift of the Spirit is a great blessing, filled with assurance and encouragement. The Spirit is a seal and earnest of our glorious inheritance in the heavenly kingdom (see 2 Cor 1:22; 5:5; 13–14). But as Christ attained his glorification only through the dark valley of the cross, so also he calls us to suffer with him in outward humility for a while, before we attain our glorification.

We saw above how Paul describes the ministry of the new covenant by the Spirit as so much more glorious than the old covenant under Moses (2 Cor 3). But any brief temptation to triumphalism quickly dissipates as we continue reading in 2 Corinthians 4. This ministry of the gospel, of which Paul is steward, has been veiled to unbelievers (2 Cor 4:3–4). Even more, the servants who proclaim this gospel of glory are weak in themselves: "God, who said, 'Let light shine out of darkness,' made his light shine in our hearts to give us the light of the knowledge of God's glory displayed in the face of Christ. But we have this treasure in jars of clay to show that this all-surpassing power is from God and not from us" (2 Cor 4:6–7). Paul describes himself and his colleagues as hard pressed, perplexed, persecuted, and struck down (2 Cor 4:8–9), but sees the pattern of Christ in this humility: "We always carry around in our body the death of Jesus, so that the life of Jesus may also be revealed in our body" (2 Cor 4:10). He finds encouragement even in these sufferings, knowing that as God raised Christ so he will also raise them (2 Cor 4:14). "Therefore we do not lose heart. Though outwardly we are wasting away, yet inwardly we are being renewed day by day. For our light and momentary troubles are achieving for us an eternal glory that far outweighs them all" (2 Cor 4:16–17).

Although Paul was primarily speaking about his own apostolic sufferings in these verses, they reflect a Christ-like pattern relevant for all Christians' experiences in this world. They put our present sufferings in perspective. For one thing, Christ's servants glorify God insofar as their lowliness testifies that the power of the gospel lies not in the human messenger but in the Lord (2 Cor 4:7). Further, it reminds us that just as the cross was Christ's path to the glory of heaven, so it is with us. Paul emphasized this point elsewhere: "If we are children, then we are heirs—heirs of God and co-heirs with Christ, if indeed we share in his sufferings in order that we may also share in his glory. I consider that our present sufferings are not worth comparing with the glory that will be revealed in us" (Rom 8:17–18).

Peter, so slow to comprehend the message of suffering-then-glory during Jesus' earthly ministry (e.g., Matt 16:21–23), learned it well later and taught it clearly in his first epistle. Jesus had explained, "Whoever wants to be my disciple must deny [himself] and take up [his] cross and follow me. For whoever wants to save [his] life will lose it, but whoever loses [his] life for me will find it" (Matt 16:24–25). Thus, Peter exhorts his readers: "Rejoice inasmuch as you participate in the sufferings of Christ, so that you may be overjoyed when his glory is revealed. If you are insulted because of the name of Christ, you are blessed, for the Spirit of glory and of God rests on you" (1 Pet 4:13–14). He expresses confidence that when this glory of Christ is revealed, he "also will share in the glory to be revealed" (1 Pet 5:1). Peter doesn't give the impression that these sufferings are anything but unpleasant in and of themselves, but he calls for joy in the midst of them in view of the coming glory. Indeed, at the head of his epistle, he set this theme before his readers: "In all this you greatly rejoice, though now for a little while you may have had to suffer grief in all kinds of trials. These have come so that the proven genuineness of your faith—of greater worth than gold, which perishes even though refined by fire—may result in praise, glory and honor when Jesus Christ is revealed" (1 Pet 1:6–7).

Here is a second crucial theme of Christians' share in Christ's glory. Like their Lord, believers must walk through the valley of the shadow of death before they dwell in the house of the Lord forever. They must suffer first, but glory awaits. And while they suffer, Christians are hardly bereft of hope and encouragement. Although hidden from the world, the glory of Christ is already at work in them by his powerful Spirit, to sustain and support them in time of trouble. Paul prayed that "out of his glorious riches," God would strengthen the Ephesians "with power through his Spirit" (Eph 3:16), and he prayed that the Colossians would be "strengthened with all power according to his glorious might," so that they might "have great endurance and patience" (Col 1:11).

Third, Christians' participation in Christ's glory, of which we have a precious though faint foretaste today, will come to brilliant completion on the day of his return. In Chapter 4 we observed how all the profound revelation of God's glory in the Old Testament—centered around the pillar of cloud and fire as it rested upon the temple, then pointing to a more glorious temple in the coming Messianic days—has found fulfillment in the heavenly Jerusalem where Christ the king, crowned with the Spirit and surrounded by the angelic host, sits enthroned. We hesitate to think that Christ's glorification could become any grander, yet this is what Scripture suggests. On the last day, Christ will return "to be glorified in his holy people and to be marveled at among all those who have believed" (2 Thess 1:10). Christ desires to be glorified not only by the one hundred million angels surrounding the throne (Rev 5:11), but also by a host of human beings, a throng of brothers and sisters whom he leads to glory (Heb 2:10–13). As Jesus prayed, just hours before his crucifixion, "Father, I want those you have given me to be with me where I am, and to see my glory, the glory you have given me because you loved me before the creation of the world" (John 17:24). Paul prayed similarly for the Thessalonians when contemplating Christ's return: "that the name of our Lord Jesus may be glorified in you, and you in him" (2 Thess 1:12). The idea of believers' glorification is not opposed to the principle of *soli Deo gloria* because our glorification redounds to the supreme glorification of our Lord.

"All have sinned and fall short of the glory of God" (Rom 3:23). This is Paul's honest assessment of the human race cursed in Adam. Glory was our God-given goal, and we failed to attain it, but in Christ God has chosen us from eternity to gain this goal at last by his grace and has called us in the midst of history to be partakers of this marvelous benefit. Chosen from eternity to attain the goal of glory—this is quite a thought, and yet thoroughly biblical. The elect, says Paul, "obtain the salvation that is in Christ Jesus, with eternal glory" (2 Tim 2:10). God ordains us to glorification from eternity, and in history calls us to the same. Paul explains that God willed to "make the riches of his glory known to the objects of his mercy, whom he prepared in advance for glory—even us, whom he also called" (Rom 9:23–24). Earlier in Romans, Paul laid the foundation for this teaching. God's people have been "called according to his purpose" (Rom 8:28). God expressed this purpose in predestining them "to be conformed to the image of his Son" (Rom 8:29). "And those he *predestined*, he also *called*; and those he called, he also *justified*; those he justified, he also *glorified*" (Rom 8:30, emphasis mine). It is an unbreakable chain.

Those God chose before time are the very ones who receive these blessings in history, culminating in glorification.

Elsewhere, Paul links glorification and the divine call. God "calls you into his kingdom and glory," he tells the Thessalonians (1 Thess 2:12). Peter blessed his readers with the same assurance: "And the God of all grace, who called you to his eternal glory in Christ, after you have suffered a little while, will himself restore you and make you strong, firm and steadfast" (1 Pet 5:10). For Peter, we are called "by his . . . glory" (2 Pet 1:3) and to his glory. So all the glory is God's.

Elected and called to heavenly glory, Christians are able to be filled with a sure hope, firm joy, and eager expectation, even in the midst of their present sufferings. Justified by faith and at peace with God, "we boast in the hope of the glory of God," a hope that enables us also to "glory in our sufferings" (Rom 5:1–3). For as we saw above, "we share in his sufferings in order that we may also share in his glory," and "our present sufferings are not worth comparing with the glory that will be revealed in us" (Rom 8:17–18). Elsewhere, Paul wished the Ephesians to know "the hope to which he has called you, the riches of his glorious inheritance in his holy people" (Eph 1:18). Hence believers need not "lose heart," even as they waste away outwardly, but fix their eyes on unseen and enduring things, that "eternal glory that far outweighs" these "light and momentary troubles" (2 Cor 4:16–18). We "rejoice" now in our fellowship in Christ's suffering, adds Peter, so that we may be "overjoyed when his glory is revealed" (1 Pet 4:13).

When precisely will this glory be revealed, and our glorification achieved? Scripture points us to Christ's second coming. Our lives are already "hidden with Christ in God," writes Paul, but "when Christ, who is your life, appears, then you also will appear with him in glory" (Col 3:3–4). As Peter puts it, the "genuineness of our faith," forged through various trials through which we rejoice, will "result in praise, glory and honor when Jesus Christ is revealed" (1 Pet 1:6–7). At this time, when the "Chief Shepherd appears," we "will receive the crown of glory that will never fade away" (1 Pet 5:4).

The resurrection of our bodies is a central aspect of our glorification at Christ's coming. As mentioned earlier, we attain certain benefits of our glorification at death—such as relief from earthly sufferings and liberation from our sinful nature—but we cannot be fully satisfied, or our glorification truly achieved, until God raises us from the dust. As Christ was raised by the Spirit and donned a glorious, Spiritual body, so will his people. The body is "sown in dishonor, it is raised in glory; it is sown in weakness, it is raised in power; it is sown a natural body, it is raised a [S]piritual body" (1 Cor 15:43–44). Knowing that we will be raised through the Spirit (Rom 8:11), we "eagerly await a Savior from [heaven], the Lord Jesus Christ, who, by the power that enables him to bring everything under his control, will transform our lowly bodies so that they will be like his glorious body" (Phil 3:20–21).

Our Lord's great return will mean "the redemption of our bodies," when finally we enjoy "the freedom and glory of the children of God" (Rom 8:21, 23). However dimly, the saints of old expected this future day: "I am always with you; you hold me by my right hand. You guide me with your counsel, and afterward you will take me into glory" (Ps 73:23–24). And now, with the promise of Christ ever in our ears—"Yes, I am coming soon" (Rev 22:20)—we praise God with Jude's doxology: "To him who is able to keep you from stumbling and to present you before his glorious presence without fault and with great joy—to the only God our Savior be glory, majesty, power and authority, through all ages, now and forevermore! Amen" (Jude 24–25)!

Doing All for the Glory of God

Earlier I noted how the theme of *soli Deo gloria*, in popular parlance, has often come to focus upon the idea that we are called to do all things for the glory of God. I claimed that although we are indeed called to do all things for God's glory, when this becomes the principal focus, we run the risk of making *soli Deo gloria* primarily about *us* and our agendas, rather than about God and his glorification of himself—an odd and ironic result. For this reason the past two and a half chapters have focused upon God and how he glorifies himself through the pillar of cloud and fire, through the humiliation and exaltation of his Son, and through the glorification of his people, among many other themes. But having laid this foundation— which surely must lie at the center of our confession that all glory belongs to God—I now turn back to this idea: God calls us to glorify him in all we do. Or perhaps to put it more precisely: one of the great ways that God glorifies himself is by calling and enabling us, his people, to glorify him through our holy conduct.

Jonathan Edwards commented, "From time to time [in Scripture], embracing and practicing true religion, and repenting of sin, and turning to holiness, is expressed by *glorifying God*, as though that were the sum and end of the whole matter."[5] If Edwards is correct, it suggests that the Christian life at heart is one of glorifying God. And if this is the case, then the specific way in which Scripture calls us to glorify God ought to provide important insight on the structure and priorities of that Christian life. We will see from Scripture that we glorify God by faith, and by the fruits of faith. Of the fruits of faith, Scripture points us repeatedly to *worship* as the primary way that Christians glorify God. Glorifying God in worship in turn spills over into all of our conduct, especially our humble works of service that build up the body of Christ. In this section we will explore these three ways—faith, worship, and humble service—by which Scripture calls us to glorify God.

First, we glorify God by our *faith*. Since our salvation in Christ comes by faith alone, and since faith is the root from which all of our good works flow (see Rom 14:23; Heb 11:6), we would expect to find an indelible connection between faith and giving glory to God in all of our conduct. Two texts, 2 Corinthians 1:20 and Romans 4:20, make this connection explicitly.

In the latter part of 2 Corinthians 1, Paul speaks at some length about his recent change of travel plans. He had notified the Corinthian church that he would be stopping by Corinth on his way to Macedonia to pay them a visit (verse 16), but then later changed his mind, for the church's own good (verse 25). Paul apparently had heard whispers that these Corinthian Christians deemed Paul's change of plans as a sign of weakness and vacillation, perhaps even of dishonesty (verse 17). In response, he emphasizes that there is really only one message that he consistently proclaims. He does not say both "yes" and no," because Jesus Christ whom he proclaims is "not 'Yes' and 'No,' but in him it has always been 'Yes.' For no matter how many promises God has made, they are 'Yes' in Christ." He then explains: "And so through him the 'Amen' is spoken by us to the glory of God" (verses 18–20). Paul uses some unusual language here that doesn't appear elsewhere in his epistles, but the meaning is evident. God made many promises to his people, and Christ is their fulfillment—he is the great Yes to God's promises of old. Paul's preaching was always Yes because it always pointed to Christ. In this light, our "Amen" can be nothing other than the act of faith. When we hear of God's promises and of Christ their Yes, the most basic and fundamental response we can offer is to say

5. Jonathan Edwards, "Concerning the End for Which God Created the World," in *Works of Jonathan Edwards*. Vol. 8, *Ethical Writings*, 479. Also see John Piper, *God's Passion for His Glory*, 196.

"Amen"—so let it be. Faith gives its assent and embraces God's promises in Christ. And how do we utter this Amen? We utter it "to the glory of God." We glorify God by faith in his promises.

The same theme is present in Romans 4. Several times in this great chapter about faith, Paul discusses Abraham, the father of all believers (see Rom 4:16). Early in the chapter he quotes Genesis 15:6, when in response to God's promise that he would have descendants as numerous as the stars in heaven, "Abraham believed God, and it was credited to him as righteousness" (Rom 4:3). Toward the chapter's end Paul returns to this incident and reflects upon the fact that Abraham was almost one hundred years old and his wife Sarah was barren. Abraham had every earthly reason to think God's promise outrageous, yet "without weakening in his faith, he faced the fact that his body was as good as dead" and "he did not waver through unbelief regarding the promise of God" (Rom 4:19–20). Instead, Paul explains, he "was strengthened in his faith and gave glory to God" (Rom 4:20).

It is not immediately clear exactly what the relationship is here between Abraham's faith and his giving glory to God, but it seems most likely that he gave glory to God precisely through this strong act of faith itself. As John Murray comments in Romans 4:20, "'Giving glory to God' and 'being fully persuaded that what he has promised he is able also to perform' are coordinate and describe the exercises or states of mind which were involved in Abraham's faith. To give glory to God is to reckon God to be what he is and to rely upon his power and faithfulness."[6] As in 2 Corinthians 1, Paul seems to see faith in the divine promises as a great act of glorifying God. Commenting on Romans 4:20, Thomas Schreiner remarks: "The essence of faith . . . is that it grants glory to God. God is glorified in faith because he is honored as the all-sufficient one who can meet every need."[7]

A second—and seemingly primary—way by which Christians glorify God is *worship*. Faith in God's Christ-centered promises gives glory to God, and thus it is no surprise to find that Scripture describes the fruits of faith—our good works—in similar terms. Are there some fruits in particular that receive special attention? Yes, there is one activity that Scripture associates far more than any other with glorifying God, and that is worship. At its heart, worship ascribes all glory to God alone. We can glorify God in many ways, but Scripture indicates that nothing we do delights

---

6.   John Murray, *The Epistle to the Romans*, vol. 1 (Grand Rapids: Eerdmans, 1959), 151.

7.   Thomas R. Schreiner, *Paul: Apostle of God's Glory in Christ: A Pauline Theology* (Downers Grove, IL: InterVarsity Press, 2001), 29.

God more than calling upon his name with sincere hearts and declaring that all glory belongs to him.

To clarify one matter initially, when I refer to "worship," I am referring to a *distinct* activity. Sometimes people speak of all of life as worship, such that going to work is worship, playing basketball is worship, or practicing the piano is worship. It is indeed proper to honor God in all of our endeavors, as we'll consider below, but worship is a distinct activity in which we set aside other tasks and set our minds and hearts fully upon the Lord, in order to receive his word and to respond to him with prayer and song—in private, in families, and especially in the corporate worship of the church on the Lord's Day. In the many biblical texts about worship mentioned in the following paragraphs, and in several more discussed in the next chapter, the repeated exhortations to call upon the Lord, sing to the Lord, praise the Lord, and other similar practices provide abundant evidence that God takes special delight in the distinct activity of worship.

Before we consider how Scripture calls us to glorify God through worship, it may be profitable to reflect for a moment on the fact that the Bible often portrays *angels* as giving glory to God in their worship. We saw this in Chapter 4 when the angels appeared to the shepherds outside Bethlehem, declaring, "Glory to God in the highest" (Luke 2:14). However, this "great company of the heavenly host" (Luke 2:13) visible on earth apparently provided just a tiny peek into the scene in heaven, where one hundred million angels encircle the throne and proclaim the Lamb worthy of all glory (Rev 5:11–12). They sing songs of praise repeatedly through the book of Revelation, and though these songs differ in detail, they often include refrains that sound something like this: "Hallelujah! Salvation and glory and power belong to our God" (Rev 19:1; cf. 5:9–12; 7:12; 15:3–4; 19:1–8).

Why is this significant? For one thing, it reminds us that God truly does delight in worship. If God is more pleased by practices other than worship, then it is very odd that worship saturates biblical descriptions of heaven. These angelic declarations of glory to God remind us that through our own worship, we join with the angelic choirs and participate even now in the heavenly ascription of glory to our Lord. This is part of the wonder of the pillar of cloud settling upon Israel's tabernacle and temple: the cloud, a replica of the heavenly court where God sits enthroned among the heavenly host, filled the place of worship on earth. The worship of the heavenly temple and the worship of the earthly temple in some marvelous way were united as one.

This helps to explain why a few of the Psalms actually exhort God's people to call upon the angels. Scripture never commands us to pray to dead *people*, but it does command us to sing to the angels. We do so not to worship them, but to encourage them to continue their worship before the heavenly throne: "Praise the LORD, you his angels, you mighty ones who do his bidding, who obey his word. Praise the LORD, all his heavenly hosts, you his servants who do his will" (Ps 103:20–21). Elsewhere, David actually urges the angels to give glory to God: "Ascribe to the LORD, you heavenly beings, ascribe to the LORD glory and strength. Ascribe to the LORD the glory due his name; worship the LORD in the splendor of his holiness" (Ps 29:1–2).

As Scripture portrays this mystical communion between human worshipers on earth and angelic worshipers in heaven, the former not only exhort the latter to keep worshiping but also seem to draw inspiration from them. Human worshipers call angels to ascribe glory to God in Psalm 29:1–2, but later in God's temple, "all cry 'Glory'" (Ps 29:9). The worshipers in the temple echo the angelic refrain. The shepherds of Bethlehem did the same thing, first hearing the angelic host declare glory to God and then going forth from the manger after seeing Jesus, "glorifying and praising God for all the things they had heard and seen" (Luke 2:14, 20). It happens again in Revelation. After John hears the first angelic song in worship of Christ—"Worthy is the Lamb, who was slain, to receive power and wealth and wisdom and strength and honor and glory and praise!"—he then hears in advance the song we all will sing when God gathers us together in the new creation: "I heard every creature in heaven and on earth and under the earth and on the sea, and all that is in them, saying: 'To him who sits on the throne and to the Lamb be praise and honor and glory and power, for ever and ever!'" (Rev 5:12–13).

When we declare God's glory in worship, we have the privilege of echoing and joining the angelic song even now, anticipating the day when our co-worshipers will be visible to our eyes and together, in one great company, we will worship the Lamb who was slain. And so we begin now, with imperfect hearts and faltering voices, to do what we will do forever: give glory to God in worship.

The theme of glorifying God in worship appears throughout the Scriptures. In the Old Testament, the godly Israelites took God's glory upon their lips. "I will praise you, Lord my God, with all my heart; I will glorify your name forever" (Ps 86:12). "One generation commends your works to another; they tell of your mighty acts. They speak of the glorious splendor of your majesty—and I will meditate on your wonderful works" (Ps 145:45).

Remarkably, Old Testament declarations of glory to God often look beyond the narrow confines of Israel. They long for a future day when all people will join their worship and the whole world will be filled with God's glory (e.g., Ps 57:9–11; 66:2; 72:19; 108:3–5; 145:10–12).

> Sing to the LORD, all the earth; proclaim his salvation day after day. Declare his glory among the nations, his marvelous deeds among all people. . . . Ascribe to the LORD, all you families of nations, ascribe to the LORD glory and strength. Ascribe to the LORD the glory due his name; bring an offering and come before him. Worship the LORD in the splendor of his holiness (1 Chr 16:23–24, 28–29; cf. Ps 96:1–3, 7–9).
>
> All the nations you have made will come and worship before you, Lord; they will bring glory to your name (Ps 86:9).
>
> May all the kings of the earth praise you, LORD, when they hear what you have decreed. May they sing of the ways of the LORD, for the glory of the LORD is great (Ps 138:4–5).

This longing is remarkable, yet vague. When will it be realized? The book of Isaiah gives some hints. On the day of final judgment, the context of Isaiah 24 suggests, people "from the west . . . [will] acclaim the LORD's majesty. Therefore in the east give glory to the LORD; exalt the name of the LORD, the God of Israel, in the islands of the sea. From the ends of the earth we hear singing: 'Glory to the Righteous One'" (Isa 24:14–16). Furthermore, in the days of the Messiah, the Servant of the Lord who brings salvation (Isa 42:1–7), God's praise will be sung from the ends of the earth, from the seas, on the islands, in the wilderness, and on the mountaintops (Isa 42:10–11)—"Let them give glory to the LORD" (Isa 42:12; cf. Isa 59:19). Isaiah finishes with a magnificent vision of the new heavens and new earth (Isa 65:17–66:24), and in this vision God declares: "I will send some of those who survive [the great coming judgment] to the nations—to Tarshish, to the Libyans and Lydians . . . to Tubal and Greece, and to the distant islands that have not heard of my fame or seen my glory. They will proclaim my glory among the nations" (Isa 66:19).

Finally, the New Testament makes clear that all of these great events— the coming of the Messiah, the final judgment, the revelation of the new heavens and new earth—do not happen simultaneously. First, the Messiah comes in humility to walk the way of the cross and then, after his gospel is preached and the church built throughout the world, the Messiah will return in glory to judge the world and to usher in the new creation. Only in the new creation will these holy Old Testament longings be truly satisfied. Only then will "every knee" bow "at the name of Jesus . . . in heaven and on earth and under the earth, and every tongue acknowledge that Jesus Christ is Lord, to the glory of God the Father" (Phil 2:10–11). Only then will "every creature in heaven and on earth and under the earth and on the sea, and all that is in them" declare glory to the Lamb (Rev 5:13). Until then, as the church is gathered through the ministry of Christ's gospel, the people of God declare God's glory in worship in ways the Old Testament saints never experienced, ways that afford an even greater foretaste of this new creation worship. Even now, throughout the whole world, Christians gather together to worship God in east and west, across the seas, on the islands, and on the mountaintops—all those places where the Old Testament prophets longed to see glory ascribed to the living God.

This great truth—that Christians give glory to God in worship, in anticipation of Christ's return—pervades the New Testament. In Luke's gospel, for example, people constantly glorify God in worship in response to the great deeds revealed in Jesus' day, beginning with the song of his mother Mary: "My soul glorifies the Lord and my spirit rejoices in God my Savior" (Luke 1:46–47). When people see Christ's miracles or receive personal benefits from them, they again and again give glory to God (see Luke 5:25–26; 7:16; 13:13; 17:15, 18; 18:43; cf. Acts 11:18; 13:48; 21:20),[8] culminating with Christ's triumphal entry into Jerusalem: "The whole crowd of disciples began joyfully to praise God in loud voices for all the miracles they had seen: 'Blessed is the king who comes in the name of the Lord! Peace in heaven and glory in the highest'" (Luke 19:37–38).

Paul calls believers to follow this pattern. For instance, immediately after reminding the Roman Christians that all good works flow from faith (Rom 14:23), Paul exhorts them to love and build up one another, following Christ's example (Rom 15:1–5), "so that with one mind and one voice you may glorify the God and Father of our Lord Jesus Christ" (Rom 15:6). After Paul portrays the glory of the new covenant in 2 Corinthians 3:6–4:14, he explains that his apostolic ministry, though veiled in suffering (2 Cor 4:7–12), is for these believers' benefit, "so that the grace that is reaching more and more people may cause thanksgiving to overflow to the glory of God" (2 Cor 4:15). The dynamic evident here in 2 Corinthians 3–4 is remarkable: Christ is the glory of God; the new covenant in Christ is glorious; the Spirit transforms believers into the image of Christ from glory

---

8. The NIV uses the word "praise" to translate the Greek word that ordinarily means "glorify."

to glory; and believers pour forth thanksgiving to God that redounds to his glory. *Soli Deo gloria*—all glory flows forth from God and returns to him.

Believers also give glory to God through worship in the New Testament by offering doxologies. "Doxology" literally means "a word of glory," and that is the perfect description of the doxologies that pervade the New Testament epistles and Revelation. Paul declares many doxologies (see Rom 16:27; Gal 1:5; Eph 3:21; Phil 4:20; 1 Tim 1:17; 2 Tim 4:18), but his most effusive is in Romans 11, which I abbreviate here: "Oh, the depth of the riches of the wisdom and knowledge of God. . . . From him and through him and for him are all things. To him be the glory forever! Amen" (Rom 11:33–36).

The author of Hebrews concludes his benediction with a similar doxology: "May he work in us what is pleasing to him, through Jesus Christ, to whom be glory for ever and ever. Amen" (Heb 13:21). Peter's second epistle closes with a doxology following a final command: "Grow in the grace and knowledge of our Lord and Savior Jesus Christ. To him be glory both now and forever! Amen" (2 Pet 3:18; cf. 1 Pet 4:11). The doxology at the end of Jude echoes Paul's in Romans 11: "To him who is able to keep you from stumbling and to present you before his glorious presence without fault and with great joy—to the only God our Savior be glory, majesty, power and authority, through Jesus Christ our Lord, before all ages, now and forevermore! Amen" (Jude 24–25). And who can forget the great doxology near the beginning of Revelation? "To him who loves us and has freed us from our sins by his blood, and has made us to be a kingdom and priests to serve his God and Father—to him be glory and power for ever and ever! Amen" (Rev 1:5–6). In light of this gracious work of Christ, these New Testament writers cannot help but ascribe glory to God, and seal their praise with the "Amen" of faith.

We've been observing the impressive depth of the pervasive biblical theme of glorifying God through worship. We come now to our third and final way in which the New Testament speaks of Christians glorifying God: glorifying God *in all that we do*. Although this is not a major theme in Scripture, contrary to what conventional wisdom might lead us to expect, the New Testament clearly does exhort us to glorify God in all of our conduct, especially that which builds up the church, the body of Christ. The pattern seems to be this: as we believe in Christ to the glory of God and declare his glory in our worship, grateful obedience in all of life flows forth from us unto God's glory, especially in works of service that bless Christ's church.

Probably the most famous text encapsulating our call to glorify God in all things is 1 Corinthians 10:31: "So whether you eat or drink or whatever you do, do it all for the glory of God." This verse sets before us a broad and challenging responsibility, although its use as a stand-alone motto risks obscuring what Paul was really trying to say. He does not mention eating and drinking because these are mundane activities and he wants believers to see that *if even eating and drinking should be done to God's glory, then surely everything should be*. Rather, he mentions eating and drinking because earlier in 1 Corinthians 10 (as well as in 1 Corinthians 8), he dealt with controversies about whether Christians are permitted to eat meat sacrificed to false gods.

In addressing this problem, Paul teaches that believers have a broad range of liberties in Christ, but he warns them not to trample on the consciences of other people who may disagree with them. They can "eat anything sold in the meat market without raising questions of conscience" (1 Cor 10:25), but should follow an even more fundamental principle: "No one should seek [his] own good, but the good of others" (1 Cor 10:24). Thus, Paul's point in 10:31 becomes evident in the next two verses: in all of our activities, including these divisive issues of eating and drinking, we should "not cause anyone to stumble, whether Jews, Greeks or the church of God—even as I try to please everyone in every way. For I am not seeking my own good but the good of many, so that they may be saved" (1 Cor 10:32–33). In short, Paul encourages us to glorify God in all things by seeking the good of all people, for the ultimate goal of seeing people saved and the church strengthened.

This ends up looking very similar to the dynamic in Romans 15:6, in the broader context of 14:1–15:13. In this text, Paul also exhorts believers to seek others' welfare when disputes arise about indifferent things, instead of seeking to please ourselves. He prays that God would give them "the same attitude of mind toward each other that Christ Jesus had" (Rom 15:5), such that God would be glorified as they worshiped him together in unity: "that with one mind and one voice you may glorify the God and Father of our Lord Jesus Christ" (Rom 15:6). The same pattern is evident in Colossians 3:13–17. Paul first exhorts to love and forgiveness toward fellow Christians, then calls them to worship, and concludes with the stirring words: "Whatever you do, whether in word or deed, do it all in the name of the Lord Jesus, giving thanks to God the Father through him" (Col 3:17).

Perhaps the most sweeping biblical text encouraging us to glorify God in all things is 1 Peter 4:10–11: "Each of you should use whatever gift you have received to serve others, as faithful stewards of God's grace in its various forms. If anyone speaks, [he] should do so as one who speaks the very words of God. If anyone serves, [he] should do so with the strength God provides, so that in all things God may be praised [literally, glorified] through Jesus Christ. To him be the glory and the power for ever and ever. Amen." Peter encourages us to use whatever gift we have, with all the strength God gives, to serve others. While he surely did not mean to limit this service to fellow Christians, his focus is upon service to our brothers and sisters in Christ, for in the previous verses he commands his readers to love "each other" and to be hospitable "to one another" (1 Pet 4:8–9). God is glorified by our whole-hearted service to others, and *especially* by our service to fellow believers.

Furthermore, Peter envisions it as a service rendered through suffering, for he goes on immediately to encourage them in their "fiery ordeal" and in suffering insults for Christ's sake (1 Pet 4:12–16). In many ways this brings us back to earlier themes of the chapter. Because the Spirit of glory rests upon us (verse 14), we may rejoice insofar as we participate in Christ's sufferings (verse 13), and may glorify God that we bear the name "Christian" (verse 16). In this context, Peter says that we should use all of our gifts for serving others, so that God is glorified in everything.

In summary, this section has highlighted three ways in which Scripture calls us to glorify God: through faith, worship, and loving service, especially toward the church. Scripture's primary emphasis upon glorifying God through worship is an important reminder of just how central worship ought to be in our Christian lives. Compared to so many other activities, worship may sometimes strike us as dull and unproductive. But while we ought never be lax in works of service to our neighbors, the texts we've considered urge us to remember that nothing glorifies the Lord more than bending the knee and calling upon his name.

Fellowship with Christ In Glory

"All saints," begins Westminster Confession of Faith 26.1, "that are united to Jesus Christ their head by his Spirit, and by faith, have fellowship with him in his . . . glory." In light of the Reformation theme of *soli Deo gloria* and the host of biblical texts that inspired it, the idea that mere creatures participate in this glory may initially strike us as contradictory, and perhaps blasphemous. But as this and the two preceding chapters have argued, Scripture does indeed say *both* that all glory belongs to God *and* that his people share in that glory. *Soli Deo gloria* is about God and how he glorifies himself, but one magnificent way God glorifies himself is through glorifying us and enabling us to glorify him through faith, worship, and whole-hearted service to him and our neighbors. What a bounteous God we have who has authored this story of divine glory and invited us to be such a vital part of it—by faith alone, by grace alone, and by Christ alone.

PART 3

Living for God's Glory Today

CHAPTER 6

Prayer and Worship in an Age of Distraction

> "What the Net seems to be doing is chipping away my capacity for concentration and contemplation . . . The Net is, by design, an interruption system, a machine geared for dividing attention." —*Nicholas Carr*

> "[H]is delight is in the law of the LORD, and on his law he meditates day and night." —*Psalm 1:2*

Chapters 3–5 examined the theme of God's glory in Scripture. Our tour of *soli Deo gloria* in God's word took us to Mount Sinai, the wilderness, and then Mount Zion, to a shepherds' field outside Bethlehem, the cross, and to the heavenly Jerusalem. It portrayed redeemed sinners as called to suffer with Christ in order that they may one day share his glory—for his glory alone. The biblical story of God's glory is in one sense timeless, calling people of all ages and in all places to participate in it through salvation in Christ. Yet in another sense, this story is deeply time-bound. The story is not a tale, after all, but *history.* God has revealed his glory in real human history, accomplished redemption in his Son in a real time and place, and will one day send his Son again to bring this world to its appointed end.

The gospel calls Christians to have a share in this grand story, to claim this story as our own. But it also calls us in our own times and places, with our own limitations and challenges. This prompts some important questions for us to consider as we reflect upon God's glory and seek to live in ways that promote it: What are the challenges of our own age? What temptations and seductions have an especially strong hold upon us as we strive to fulfill our chief calling, to glorify and enjoy God? What things should make us especially vigilant?

In asking such questions, we need to be circumspect. As Paul said,

"No temptation has overtaken you except what is common to mankind" (1 Cor 10:13). Because our fundamental problem as human beings is our sinful hearts, rather than particular temptations in our surrounding culture, no evil that seduces us today is brand new. The vices that orient us away from virtuous character and toward sinful conduct are perennial. Nevertheless, the assumptions and customs of our ambient cultures do shape us in powerful ways, often in ways we scarcely realize. Although we shouldn't blithely act as though our own cultural challenges are *unique*, they are often distinctive. The way of wisdom instructs us to be attentive to near and present temptations and to be on our guard against their subtle seductions, which can pull us away from a God-glorifying life.

Perhaps the phenomenon that most distinctly characterizes our age—at least in First World countries, but rapidly in so many others as well—is the rise of the Internet and the numerous gadgets, mass communications, instant data, and social media it has enabled and inspired. The benefits of this new technology are so numerous that it seems pedantic to list them. But we are especially interested here in asking whether it also brings with it peculiar challenges and temptations that hinder Christians from pursuing faithful service to God, and particularly from seeking God's glory. The answer is clearly Yes. A very serious set of challenges involves the way the new technology tends to multiply distractions and even to wire a state of constant distractedness into our hearts and minds. This distractedness, in turn, tends to discourage deep contemplation and to promote shallow thinking instead.

Of course, being distracted is not sinful per se, and we may be tempted to dismiss deep contemplation as only the province of professional scholars. But in fact, there is at least one area of life in which focused attention and deep reflection are crucial for *all* Christians: worship and prayer. God is not honored (and we ourselves are little edified) by worship rendered with distracted hearts and minds unwilling—or even unable—to probe "the depth of the riches of the wisdom and knowledge of God" (Rom 11:33). We saw in the previous chapter that Scripture on many occasions speaks about Christians glorifying God, and it envisions Christians doing so above all through worship. Thus, to the extent that our new technology pushes us to distraction and threatens to hinder our ability to concentrate and to dig deeply into worthy matters, it behooves us to be on guard against its encroachment into the whole of life.

This chapter first considers the importance of worship, meditation, and prayer for the Christian life—and the importance of practicing them not just formally but with engaged minds and hearts. Then, I will discuss how our new technologies are shaping our customs, and even our brains, in ways that encourage distracted, shallow thinking. I conclude by turning back to matters of prayer and worship, reflecting on how we might fortify ourselves in the face of contemporary challenges and be built up in focused attention and deep contemplation as we call upon the Lord, for his glory.

The Centrality of Prayer and Worship for the Christian Life

It would be difficult to exaggerate the importance of prayer for Reformation Christianity, and for the Reformed tradition in particular. This may be surprising to some people. In a religion that emphasizes the sovereignty of God and the salvation of fallen sinners by his grace alone in Christ alone, why would prayer be important or necessary? It is clear that the Reformed view of God and his graciously sovereign salvation inspired not indifference toward prayer but a conviction that it is of prime importance in the Christian life.

The sixteenth-century Heidelberg Catechism, still one of Reformed Christians' most beloved teaching tools today, illustrates this poignantly. The Heidelberg Catechism is divided into three main sections: the first discusses our sin and misery, the second our gracious salvation in Christ, and the third our grateful response to God's grace. In the midst of the third section, Question 116 asks why Christians need to pray. The answer begins, "Because prayer is the most important part of the thankfulness God requires of us."[1] What a remarkable statement. The center of the third part of the catechism states that *prayer* is the most important part of our gratitude to God. This is no aberration in the history of Reformed theology. Early in John Calvin's discussion of prayer in his *Institutes of the Christian Religion*, he wrote: "The necessity and utility of this exercise of prayer no words can sufficiently express."[2] To learn that God, the giver of all good gifts, invites us to make requests of him, and then in response *not* to pray, Calvin adds, is "just as if one told of a treasure were to allow it to remain buried in the ground."[3]

Why have Reformed theologians spoken so highly of prayer's importance? We observed a key reason in the previous chapter: God made us to

---

1. Translations of the Heidelberg Catechism in this chapter are taken from *Ecumenical Creeds and Reformed Confessions* (Grand Rapids: CRC Publications, 1988).
2. Calvin, *Institutes*, 3.20.2.
3. Ibid., 3.20.1.

glorify him, and we glorify him chiefly by calling upon him in prayer (and other acts of worship). Seventeenth-century Reformed theologian Herman Witsius wrote, "With regard to God, prayer is a most important part of that worship by which he commands us to do him honor. . . . It is evident from the nature of the subject, that holy prayers render the highest possible honor to God."[4]

Secondarily, prayer also is of great benefit to ourselves. Witsius writes, "If . . . we look at ourselves, a wide view of the necessity and advantage of prayer is instantly opened. In ourselves we are in want of all things, so that, unless supported by divine aid, we cannot subsist for a moment."[5] We can see here why the Reformed emphasis on God's gracious sovereignty in salvation bolsters, rather than hinders, a high view of prayer: we are so terribly needy. If we were self-sufficient and able to bless ourselves with life and salvation, we would have little need to pray. As it is, we are weak and helpless sinners who have no hope in ourselves, and thus nothing could be more fitting than that we call out to God to bring us aid. Similarly, the end of Heidelberg Catechism 116 states that we need to pray "because God gives his grace and Holy Spirit only to those who pray continually and groan inwardly, asking God for these gifts and thanking him for them." In other words, God is sovereign over salvation, but he works through means, and prayer is a chief means by which he bestows salvation's benefits. No one can expect God's saving grace without it.

To this point I have been using some general terms—especially prayer and worship—that I have not defined. Technically speaking, worship is a broader term than prayer, for while prayer is an essential aspect of worship, worship consists of more than prayer alone. Yet we sometimes use "prayer" as shorthand for worship, as Jesus himself did in calling the temple a "house of prayer" (Mark 11:17). Trying to define various terms precisely is not my interest, but it is worth thinking briefly about several of the ways in which God wishes us to worship and pray.

The most important of all is corporate worship. By corporate worship I mean the formal worship we render as the church, the body of Christ's people, especially on the Sabbath. One reason to see this as the most important form of worship is because Scripture describes the worship of heaven as corporate in nature. As noted in the previous chapter, Revelation constantly portrays the angelic host as rendering worship to

---

4.   Herman Witsius, *Sacred Dissertations on the Lord's Prayer*, trans. William Pringle (1839; republished Escondido, CA: The den Dulk Christian Foundation, 1994), 51, 53.
5.   Ibid., 54.

God by ascribing all glory to him (e.g., Rev 5:9–12; 7:12; 15:3–4; 19:1–8). Likewise, Hebrews describes the heavenly Jerusalem as a worshiping assembly including both angels and believers who have been "made perfect" (Heb 12:22–23). Scripture never describes angels or humans in heaven as tucked away in their own private corners offering solitary prayer, but as joining their voices together in corporate adoration to God. Hebrews refers to "thousands upon thousands of angels" and to the "*church* of the firstborn, whose *names* are written in heaven" (Heb 12:22–23). Revelation expands the ranks to include "ten thousand times ten thousand" angels (Rev 5:11). Heaven is above all a place of worship, and more specifically a place of corporate worship.

As I suggested in the previous chapter, our ascription of glory to God in worship here on earth anticipates and even now is part of heavenly worship. What we will be doing in heaven perfectly forever we begin doing, however imperfectly, here on earth. This is surely why God takes such great delight in our glorifying him through worship now, and why we rightly see worship—and particularly corporate worship—as the chief way we glorify and enjoy him.

This emphasis on glorifying God through corporate worship is not just theoretical or merely a logical deduction from biblical descriptions of heaven. The Old Testament law required Israel to gather corporately for sacred festivals (see Num 28–29). In his earthly ministry, Jesus worshiped at synagogues on the Sabbath as his regular custom (e.g., Luke 4:16) and also observed the annual festivals in Jerusalem (e.g., John 2:13; 5:1; 7:10; 10:10). God established the New Testament church on the Day of Pentecost, in the midst of a corporate gathering (Acts 2:1–4), and the first converts devoted themselves to corporate worship (Acts 2:42). Later converts in the book of Acts did the same. Paul was concerned about maintaining propriety in public worship (e.g., 1 Cor 11, 14) and Hebrews specifically forbids believers from "giving up meeting together" (Heb 10:25). Corporate worship, for a variety of reasons, lies at the heart and soul of the Christian life.

But private worship is also an important forum for glorifying God, in families and individually, both through meditating on Scripture and prayer. With regard to Scripture, we might think of the blessed man in Psalm 1: his "delight is in the law of the LORD," and he "meditates on his law day and night" (Ps 1:2). This psalm clearly has more than a corporate use of God's Word in mind, for it portrays the blessed man as continually pondering God's law in his heart. Another psalmist puts it memorably:

"I have hidden your word in my heart that I might not sin against you" (Ps 119:11). How has he hidden God's Word in his heart? He explains: "I meditate on your precepts and consider your ways. I delight in your decrees; I will not neglect your word" (Ps 119:15–16).

These biblical texts and others like them do not explicitly command the *reading* of Scripture privately, and indeed it really could not have done so, since most of God's people had no access to books before the days of modern publishing. What his saints did, however, was to memorize, treasure, and ponder God's Word that they had heard read and explained to them. In our own day, insofar as Christians long to hide God's Word in their hearts and delight in it, it is difficult to imagine how we would not take up the Scriptures, so readily accessible in our own languages, and read them thoughtfully on a regular basis. And if we seek to instruct our children in the ways of the Lord, as Scripture also commands us (e.g., Ps 48:12–13; Prov 22:6; Eph 6:4), this private Bible reading should also be a regular family activity. In an age when Scripture is so widely available, the Westminster Larger Catechism does well to urge that "all sorts of people are bound to read it apart by themselves, and with their families."[6]

God calls his people not only to private meditation on Scripture but also to private prayer. Again, the Psalms provide rich material for reflection. The psalmists often speak of crying out to the Lord and calling upon his name. "I call out to the LORD, and he answers me from his holy mountain" (Ps 3:4); "Answer me when I call to you, my righteous God. Give me relief from my distress; have mercy on me and hear my prayer" (Ps 4:1); "Listen to my words, LORD, consider my lament. Hear my cry for help, my King and my God, for to you I pray" (Ps 5:1–3). And these examples only take us through the first five psalms. In the New Testament, Paul exhorts: "Devote yourselves to prayer, being watchful and thankful" (Col 4:2); and "pray continually, give thanks in all circumstances; for this is God's will for you in Christ Jesus" (1 Thess 5:17–18). By such conduct Christians imitate the Lord Jesus, who often went off alone to pray to his heavenly Father (e.g., Luke 11:1).

Thus far we've seen that we ought to pray and worship, both publicly as the church and privately as families and individuals. That raises a subsequent question: *how* are we to perform these activities? A complete answer to this question would involve discussion of the outward form and content of worship. Traditionally, Reformed Christianity has affirmed that God should be

---

6. *Westminster Larger Catechism*, 156.

worshiped only in ways he has established in Scripture,[7] and that we should pray only "for things agreeable to his will."[8] The new technologies pose plenty of challenges for maintaining proper outward forms of worship. The new technologies' emphases upon speed, efficiency, multitasking, multimedia presentation, and the like tend to make many characteristic features of Reformed worship—for example, pastoral prayers, the singing of psalms and hymns, sermons, the celebration of the Lord's Supper, and gathering to do these things in simple, unadorned rooms—seem quaint and boring in comparison. The church has always struggled with the temptation to add things to worship beyond what God has ordained in Scripture, and the seductions are stronger than ever in an Internet age.

These matters are very important, but are not our chief concern here. In the rest of this chapter, I wish to focus not upon the outward form and content but upon the inner mind and heart by which we pray, insofar as the new technologies that surround us threaten to erode the virtues of mind and heart necessary for God-pleasing worship.

How, then, are we to pray and worship in an inwardly proper manner? When question 117 of the Heidelberg Catechism asks what kind of prayer pleases God, its answer begins, "We must pray from the heart." In its description of proper prayer, the Westminster Confession of Faith urges us to pray "with understanding, reverence, humility, fervency, faith, love, and perseverance."[9] To put it in my own words, pious prayer that brings glory to God must be *focused* and it must be *deep*.

Prayer and worship must be *focused* because hearts that are inattentive and wandering here and there while supposedly calling upon God dishonor him rather than glorify him. This was one of the many charges that God brought against the Israelites. Even when they maintained outwardly proper forms of worship, their hearts' devotion failed to match their mouths' confession. Most famously, God said: "These people come near to me with their mouth and honor me with their lips, but their hearts are far from me" (Isa 29:13). Jesus borrowed these same words to condemn the religious leaders of his own day (Matt 15:7–9). Isaiah and Christ were undoubtedly condemning hypocritical unbelievers, people who did not in fact have true faith. But these words also provide an important warning for

---

7.   E.g., see *Westminster Confession of Faith* 21.1: "The acceptable way of worshiping the true God is instituted by himself, and so limited by his own revealed will, that he may not be worshiped according to the imaginations and devices of men, or the suggestions of Satan, under any visible representation, or any other way not prescribed in the Holy Scriptures."

8.   *Westminster Shorter Catechism*, 98.

9.   *Westminster Confession of Faith*, 21.3.

believers: God wants the desires of our hearts to correspond to the words of our mouths. Believers do not glorify God when they come before him in prayer while their minds are elsewhere—thinking not only about sinful things but about extraneous matters.

As Witsius observed, "The mind, unquestionably, is of chief importance in prayer."[10] He explains: "As prayer is a conversation between the soul and God, that prayer ought to be considered as the best which is the simplest, and which expresses most briefly the pious desires produced by the Holy Spirit. Its principal object ought to be, that the mind of the suppliant may be laid open to God in all its recesses, so that God may not only hear the prayers as they are expressed in language, but may see them as they are formed in the heart."[11] Calvin remarks: "Let the first rule of right prayer then be, to have our heart and mind framed as becomes those who are entering into converse with God. This we shall accomplish in regard to the mind, if . . . it not only be wholly intent on prayer, but also, as far as possible, be borne and raised above itself."[12] Later, he adds:

> First, let every one in professing to pray turn thither all his thoughts and feelings, and be not (as is usual) distracted by wandering thoughts. . . . No man is so intent on prayer as not to feel many thoughts creeping in, and either breaking off the tenor of his prayer, or retarding it by some turning or digression. Here let us consider how unbecoming it is when God admits us to familiar intercourse, to abuse his great condescension by mingling things sacred and profane, reverence for him not keeping our minds under restraint; but just as if in prayer we were conversing with one like ourselves, forgetting him, and allowing our thoughts to run to and fro.[13]

Our prayer and worship should be *deep* as well as focused. In saying this, I do not suggest that the prayers of ordinary Christians need to be as doctrinally profound as what a learned theologian may offer. But God does wish every Christian, in the words of Peter, to "grow in the grace and knowledge of our Lord and Savior Jesus Christ" (2 Pet 3:18). Paul's wish in Ephesians 3:18–19 was not intended for professional theologians but for "all the Lord's holy people": that we "may have power . . . to grasp how wide and long and high and deep is the love of Christ, and to know this love that surpasses knowledge." As Paul exhorts elsewhere,

---

10. Witsius, *The Lord's Prayer*, 34.
11. Ibid., 57–58.
12. Calvin, *Institutes*, 3.20.4–5.
13. Ibid., 3.20.4–5.

let the word of Christ "dwell among you richly as you teach and admonish one another" (Col 3:16). When we consider that Christians grow in the grace and knowledge of Christ precisely through the activities we are considering here—corporate worship and private prayer and meditation on Scripture—it seems clear that we cannot be satisfied with a cursory and surface engagement with the great truths of the faith. We meditate on God's word so that our understanding of Christ and our life in him might expand; we pray so that our communion with the living God might be deepened. In these ways God is glorified.

If this is how we are to approach God in worship, then Christians must be on guard against anything that inhibits God-glorifying worship by promoting distraction and shallow thinking. But it is becoming increasingly clear that this is precisely what our new technologies tend to do.

Distracted and Shallow: Challenges to Worship in an Internet Age

In this section, I reflect upon the new technology that has emerged alongside the formation of the Internet, including the proliferation of electronic devices that access it and the various forms of social media that utilize it. This new technology presents significant challenges for contemporary Christians through its tendency to promote customary behavior and even patterns of thinking that inhibit focused attention and deep contemplation. Such attention and contemplation, we have seen, are fundamental characteristics of godly worship and prayer. As mentioned at the beginning of the chapter, my interest is not at all to steer Christians away from use of these new technologies altogether. But as with all cultural developments and technological advances at any time in history, Christians are called to be vigilant in their use of it and careful about subtle ways in which the subsequent patterns of conduct in the world around us may obstruct our devotion to Christ. Paul encourages the saints in Romans 12:2: "Do not conform to the pattern of this world, but be transformed by the renewing of your mind."

In this spirit, Christians should desire to use new technologies in godly and productive ways. There is obviously no one right way to use them. But given their tendencies to promote distraction and shallow thinking, I will suggest in the last section of this chapter that Christians do need to moderate their use of them for the sake of their chief calling in life—to glorify God—and for the sake of the chief way they fulfill that calling: deep and attentive worship.

The first characteristic of the new technologies to consider here is the way they foster a general culture of distraction. The evidence is all around us, and most readers can offer testimony from their own lives. Our smartphones are usually—perhaps always—on, signaling with rings, beeps, and vibrations not only incoming calls but also newly received texts and emails. While doing something productive on our laptops, we're always one click away from checking email, searching the web, or visiting a favorite social media site (Facebook, Twitter, etc.). When trying to read something posted on a website, pervasive links to other sites lure us in other directions. People text while driving and talk on the phone while sitting on the toilet. Nicholas Carr, an astute observer of the effects of our new technologies, understandably refers to "the permanent state of distractedness that defines the online life." "The Net," he adds, "is, by design, an interruption system, a machine geared for dividing attention."[14]

One of the correlates of our distracted modern lives is the embrace of multitasking. Efficient, driven people have long tried to do several things at once, but while the spellchecker on my word-processing program recognizes the term "multitask," my well-worn Webster's dictionary, which I received as a high school graduation gift twenty-five years ago, does not include the word. Apparently the Internet age compelled us to invent it. Many people boast about their multitasking abilities, but as a recent writer has observed, "It's not really that you multitask, it's that your brain oscillates between two activities."[15] Or as another author puts it: "Multitasking is essentially the juggling of interruptions. . . . We spend a great deal of our days trying to piece our thoughts and our projects back together, and the result is often an accumulation of broken pieces with a raggedy coherence all its own."[16]

It is not as if distraction, or even multitasking, has never before been a problem for human beings. In previous ages, crying children diverted conversations, rainstorms interrupted work, and wandering thoughts broke off leisurely reflection. Distractions have always been part of life. But compare the opportunities for distraction for someone in days past laboring by himself in a field with the opportunities for distraction of many modern

---

14. Nicholas Carr, *The Shallows: What the Internet Is Doing to Our Brains* (New York: Norton, 2010), 112, 131. Maggie Jackson refers to our "cultivating a culture of distraction." See *Distracted: The Erosion of Attention and the Coming Dark Age* (Amherst, NY: Prometheus, 2008), 19.

15. Catherine Steiner-Adair, *The Big Disconnect: Protecting Childhood and Family Relationships in the Digital Age* (New York: HarperCollins, 2013), 58, quoting Dimitri Christakis.

16. Jackson, *Distracted*, 84.

workers with multiple electronic devices within arm's reach. The difference is enormous. The ready availability of these devices and the cultural pressure to keep up with all the news and information they provide mean, at the very least, that these new technologies threaten to build habits of distraction in us. Even more disconcerting is the growing evidence that such change in habits is not simply a spiritual or ethereal change, but entails actual modifications in our brains and the way they operate.

Some people claim that as long as the content of a message remains the same, it really doesn't matter what medium communicates it. This is almost surely wrong. As Carr notes, "In the long run a medium's content matters less than the medium itself in influencing how we think and act. As our window onto the world, and onto ourselves, a popular medium molds what we see and how we see it—and eventually, if we use it enough, it changes who we are." Hence, he continues, "Media aren't just channels of information. They supply the stuff of thought, but they also shape the process of thought."[17] Carr summarizes some of the findings of recent brain science about the phenomenon of plasticity. "Virtually all of our neural circuits," he explains, "—whether they're involved in feeling, seeing, hearing, moving, thinking, earning, perceiving, or remembering—are subject to change." Thus, "as particular circuits in our brain strengthen through the repetition of a physical or mental activity, they begin to transform that activity into a habit."[18]

What sorts of changes to our brains, and hence our thinking abilities, actually result from the near constant use of the new technologies on the part of so many people, including Christians? Carr speaks personally of what he tries to establish more objectively elsewhere: "What the Net seems to be doing is chipping away my capacity for concentration and contemplation. Whether I'm online or not, my mind now expects to take in information the way the Net distributes it: in a swiftly moving stream of particles."[19]

Carr makes his case broader by surveying an earlier historical shift in the way people know and think, one that moved in the opposite direction. This shift was spawned by the development of reading and writing and then especially by modern publishing and the widespread literacy that ensued. Carr argues that these developments encouraged the growth of deep thinking in all sorts of ways. People (immersed in their books) and

17. Carr, *The Shallows*, 3, 6.
18. Ibid., 26, 34.
19. Carr, *The Shallows*, 6–7. See also Steiner-Adair, *The Big Disconnect*, 58.

authors (writing for such readers) became better able to develop, understand, and evaluate important claims. Libraries and educational systems
emerged that were designed to fit such an intellectual culture.[20] "As our
ancestors imbued their minds with the discipline to follow a line of argument or narrative through a succession of printed pages, they became more
contemplative, reflective, and imaginative."[21]

While our own days are still filled with writing and reading, Carr
argues that the new technologies work against the contemplation and
reflection that the older world of printed material fostered. "The pathways
in our brains," he says, "are once again being rerouted."[22] He notes how
the shift from paper to screen both changes the way we navigate written
material and "influences the degree of attention we devote to it and the
depth of our immersion in it." Hyperlinks within electronic texts can be
valuable, yet by nature they encourage "us to dip in and out of a series
of texts rather than devote sustained attention to any one of them." A
search engine, again so useful for many things, "often draws our attention
to a particular snippet of text, a few words or sentences that have strong
relevance to whatever we're searching for at the moment, while providing
little incentive for taking in the work as a whole."[23] E-books are perhaps
the new media's best hope of maintaining and advancing the sort of deep
reading encouraged by the advent of easy printing and widespread literacy.
But even these tend to become more like web sites than printed books due
to their various digital enhancements, Carr argues.[24] In short, "when we
go online, we enter an environment that promotes cursory reading, hurried
and distracted thinking, and superficial learning. It's possible to think
deeply while surfing the Net . . . , but that's not the type of thinking the
technology encourages and rewards."[25]

One other feature of Carr's work may be helpful to highlight: the
importance of long-term memory for deep understanding and the baleful
effects that our new technologies tend to have on this aspect of our mind.
One of the benefits of the new technologies, it may seem, is to provide a
substitute for the frailties of our finite and very fallible memories. Isn't
long-term memory much less important when we have so much information at our fingertips and can preserve so many of our own experiences in

20. See Carr, *The Shallows*, chapters 3–4.
21. Carr, *The Shallows*, 75.
22. Ibid., 77.
23. Ibid., 90–91.
24. Ibid., 103–04.
25. Ibid., 115–16.

our mass of photos and emails? Whatever the benefits of having so much accessible information, it can never in fact be a good substitute for the memories stored in our own brains. Long-term memory, Carr points out, "is actually the seat of understanding. It stores not just facts but complex concepts, or 'schemas.' By organizing scattered bits of information into patterns of knowledge, schemas give depth and richness to our thinking." When we don't effectively transfer information from our short-term working memory to our long-term memory, "our ability to learn suffers, and our understanding remains shallow."[26]

The contemporary challenge is that distraction hinders this ability to make short-term memories long-term memories.[27] "The key to memory consolidation is attentiveness. Storing explicit memories and, equally important, forming connections between them requires strong mental concentration, amplified by repetition or by intense intellectual or emotional engagement."[28] Hence the deleterious effects of too much use of the new technologies: "The influx of competing messages that we receive whenever we go online not only overloads our working memory; it makes it much harder for our frontal lobes to concentrate our attention on any one thing. The process of memory consolidation can't even get started."[29] As Maggie Jackson, another commentator on new technologies, remarks, "Depending too heavily on multitasking to navigate a complex environment and on technology as our guide carries a final risk: the derailing of the painstaking work of adding to our storehouses of knowledge. . . . Attention helps us understand and make sense of the world and is crucial as a first step to creating memory. But more than simply attending is necessary. 'We must also process it at an abstract, schematic, conceptual level.' . . . This involves both rote repetition and 'elaborative rehearsal,' or meaningfully relating it to other information, preferably not too quickly To build memory is to construct a treasure trove of experience, wisdom, and pertinent information."[30]

These concerns regarding distraction and shallow thinking call Christians to be alert to what new technologies are doing to us, especially in light of our chief calling to glorify God through attentive worship and probing prayer. To the extent we are shaping the habits of our hearts and even structures of our brains in ways that make concentration and

26. Ibid., 124–25.
27. Ibid., 184.
28. Ibid., 193.
29. Ibid., 194.
30. Jackson, *Distracted*, 94.

contemplation more difficult—even when we are away from our electronic devices—Christians have urgent reason to reform their ways.

This is true for all of us old enough to be responsible for our behavior, and those of us who are parents have the additional responsibility to guard our children from these dangers and to train them in practices that build skills of concentration and contemplation. It is difficult enough for adults to be sufficiently aware of how modern media affects our thoughts and habits—how much more so for our young and inexperienced children who have never lived without the Internet and its trappings. Yet, as Catherine Steiner-Adair observes, we hand "these devices—that we use the language of addiction to describe—over to our children, who are even more vulnerable to problems of use and abuse and the impact of everyday use on their developing brains. . . . In our enthusiasm to be early adapters, and to give our kids every advantage, are we putting our children in harm's way?" Later, she laments: "Research already points to serious concerns for infant and child development, neurological effects that are narrowing the way the baby brain organizes for lifelong learning. Yet we place tech in the hands of infants and young children and encourage them to play."[31] If our own personal responsibility to glorify God through devoted, heartfelt worship is not incentive enough to soberly consider our use of new technologies, perhaps the desire to see our children walk thoughtfully and devoutly before the Lord will add the needed motivation.

With All of Our Heart: Worshiping the Lord with Attentive Devotion

Faced with this cultural ethos that pushes us toward distraction and shallow thinking, faithful Christian living compels us to redouble our commitment to the glorification of God by praying and worshiping with focused attention and deep understanding. Praying and worshiping God with devout fidelity has always been difficult for sinful people, and Satan has always delighted in distracting believers from these blessed activities. But our present cultural atmosphere compounds the challenges.[32]

Christians have always needed an interconnected set of virtues in order to pray well. Virtues refer to character traits, but character traits can be good or bad; we refer to these, respectively, as virtues and vices. One way

---

31. Steiner-Adair, *The Big Disconnect*, 6, 25.

32. For extensive discussion of many other aspects of the Christian life in light of modern technology and its distractions, see also Tim Challies, *The Next Story: Life and Faith After the Digital Explosion* (Grand Rapids: Zondervan, 2011).

to summarize the previous section is to say that our new technologies tend to promote certain vices that hinder our ability to worship properly. What we need to do, therefore, is strive against these influences of contemporary culture by cultivating the virtues that promote godly prayer.

What are these virtues that promote faithful prayer and worship? I cannot try to be comprehensive here, but we can consider several that are certainly crucial. One of them is *self-control*. Just as we need self-control to resist impulses toward unlawful use of food, drink, sex, and words, so we need it to resist impulses toward wandering thought during prayer. Jackson does not write from a Christian perspective, but she recognizes how important this virtue is against the vice the ancient Greeks called *akrasia*, impulsivity rooted in a weak will. "Self-control is a complex and fascinating concept that is central to fostering the reflective thinking skills and deep engagement in learning that are so needed, individually and collectively, in the digital age." She refers particularly to "attention control."[33] The apostle Paul, of course, listed self-control as the final fruit of the Spirit (Gal 5:23).

Another fruit of the Spirit, *patience*, and its companion, *perseverance*, are also essential. There is almost nothing worth achieving in this world that does not take time and involve obstacles to be overcome. Becoming skilled at playing a musical instrument or in an athletic endeavor, for example, requires years of practice and provokes numerous temptations to quit. Relationships with family and friends develop over extended periods, and demand time, sacrifice, tolerance, and long-suffering. The same is true of our relationship with God. Sanctification—our growth in holiness—is a lifelong process that remains imperfect until we reach heavenly glory. Central to this growth is corporate worship, meditation on Scripture, and faithful prayer, all of which we considered at the opening of this chapter. But we are often tempted to discouragement, boredom, and doubt in our worship. Only patience and perseverance enables us to continue waiting upon the Lord in the midst of these obstacles.[34]

Quentin Schultze also mentions *intimacy* as an important practice often sacrificed to "observation" in our technological age. While we may not think of intimacy as a virtue per se, Schultze is right to warn us about becoming people marked by superficiality: "Information technologies

---

33. Jackson, *Distracted*, 230–31.
34. Quentin J. Schultze helpfully calls attention to the importance of these virtues in his study of the new technologies and Christian character, *Habits of the High-Tech Heart: Living Virtuously in the Information Age* (Grand Rapids: Baker Academic, 2002), 26, 57.

foster secondhand knowledge *about* rather than more intimate knowledge *of*," and they tend to stress "the instrumental value of accessing information over the intrinsic good in knowing well."[35] While Schultze refers to knowledge of information in these statements, it can apply just as well to knowledge of people. Online relationships can really never enjoy the depth of intimacy that face-to-face relationships can, cultivated over years and decades. If we become people increasingly accustomed to the more superficial relationships sustained by email, texts, and Facebook, we are in danger of losing our ability to cultivate the most important intimate relationship we can ever have: our relationship with God. As John says, we cannot be lovers of God unless we are lovers of our fellow human beings (1 John 4:20).

It is one thing to identify some of the virtues we are in particular danger of losing in our day, but another thing actually to cultivate them. How can we grow in these and other virtues that encourage concentration and deep thinking, which in turn aid us to be faithful worshipers of the living God? First and foremost, we ask God to shape our hearts in this direction. God himself, by his Spirit through the word, is our sanctifier (1 Thess 5:23). As he alone regenerates us and brings life to our dead souls (Ezek 36:26; Eph 2:5; 1 Pet 1:23), and as he alone works faith in us as a gift (Phil 1:29), so he alone can produce the fruits of regeneration and faith in our Christian walk (Ezek 36:27). We are radically dependent upon God, and we cry out to him to work self-control, patience, perseverance, and all other virtues within us. For Christians discouraged by besetting sins and weak in the face of temptations, it is great comfort to know that God does not leave us to sanctify ourselves. *He* is our sanctifier.

As we beseech God's help, however, we are not to sit around passively. Scripture constantly calls us to put off the old ways of sin and to strive after holiness. While God is our sanctifier, he carries out this work only in the context of our own battles against temptation. As John Murray put it, "It is imperative that we realize our complete dependence upon the Holy Spirit. We must not forget, of course, that our activity is enlisted to the fullest extent in the process of sanctification."[36] By nature, human beings build habits, whether good or bad, by repeated conduct over periods of time. Character traits become ingrained in us through practice. Since the Spirit sanctifies us as human beings—not as some other kind of creature—he builds virtues in us over time as we pursue practices that accustom our

35. Schultze, *Habits of the High-Tech Heart*, 31–32.
36. John Murray, *Redemption: Accomplished and Applied*, 183.

hearts and minds to wholesome desires. Thus, we ought to ponder what sorts of practices we should be pursuing in order to foster the virtues that support God-glorifying prayer and worship.

In general, it is important that we conduct the *non*-praying and *non*-worshiping parts of our lives in ways conducive to building worship-friendly virtues. At a basic level, wisdom suggests that we need to leave periods of time in our lives when we are not connected to our electronic devices and not trying madly to multitask. If being connected and multitasking, by their natures, tend to promote distractedness, shallow thinking, and superficial relationships, then we need to clear space in our lives for their absence.

What are healthy things to put in their place? Spending good time with friends and family is an excellent place to start. And this means not simply being in the same room with them, but each person laying aside his or her smartphone and engaging in activities together—especially having conversations with one another, since good conversational skills are another common casualty of our new technologies, particularly among children.[37] One of the best places to spend time together in meaningful conversation is the table. Eating meals together is one of the best ways families can build and maintain their relationships, although this takes considerable effort in many contemporary homes where parents and children are so busy. Another excellent thing to fill the time when we are not connected and not multitasking is in-depth reading. Many people do read often, but seldom get beyond cursory skimming of anything in particular. Taking some time to read articles or books—and to read them deliberately, thoughtfully, and even all the way to the end—develops (or in some cases re-develops) our minds in ways wonderfully fitted to devout worship. And doing so at least some of the time with a printed text, rather than on a screen, may help to alleviate the temptations to divert our attention to other texts or forms of entertainment while we're trying to read.

Another practice that supports God-glorifying worship is observing the Sabbath. Observing the Sabbath, in fact, provides a double bonus. For one thing, the Sabbath serves as a built-in break from the regular routines of life that get so crowded with work and the constant connectedness of our new technologies. At creation, God established the pattern of six days of work followed by a day of rest, and he blessed and hallowed the seventh day (Gen 1:1–2:3). At Sinai, God commanded the Israelites to follow this pattern by structuring their week according to the six-and-one pattern.

---

37. E.g., see Steiner-Adair, *The Big Disconnect*, 61–62.

Under the new covenant, Jesus rose from the dead on Sunday, the first day of the week (John 20:1), and established a modified pattern for Christians to structure their week: not six-and-one but one-and-six. Jesus met with his disciples on Sundays (John 20:19, 26), and the early church gathered on Sundays for worship (Acts 20:7; 1 Cor 16:2). The shift of days is a wonderful testimony that we do not work first in order to earn a rest from God, but rather God gives us rest as a free gift and then calls us to take up our work in gratitude.

While most Christians continue to acknowledge the importance of setting aside an hour or so for public worship on Sundays, few show much interest in honoring Sunday as a *day* of worship and rest. It is difficult to estimate how much of a loss this is. From the beginning, God communicated to us the wisdom of resting one whole day in seven, and now—when so many of us feel overwhelmed by crazy busy, multitasking modern lives—Christians often find it a challenge to pause for an hour a week. If anything, our cluttered modern lives surely make a day of rest all the more important for us today, part of God's own remedy for healing the distractedness and superficiality that plague us.

With the demands of work, children, and ever-beckoning electronic devices, many Christians find it almost unimaginable that they could really set aside their regular routines for one day out of seven. But while there are "works of necessity" that we cannot and should not neglect on Sunday, Christians have often discovered that when they responsibly order "their common affairs beforehand," they are indeed able to clear Sunday from much of the clutter and busyness of Monday through Saturday.[38] When they do, they realize that observing the Sabbath is not a burden, but a gift from God. Many secular writers call for times of quiet, peace, and contemplation to combat the distractedness and shallowness promoted by our new technologies,[39] but Christians may be grateful that God has established a whole day every week for us to enjoy such rest—without any need to feel guilty about it.

That leads us to the second aspect of the double bonus: honoring the Sabbath provides open space for serious and unhurried worship, the very activities that ought to be most precious to us. When the time of corporate worship is bounded not by the busyness and connectedness of ordinary life but by a broader day of rest, Christians can enjoy corporate worship feeling less pressed by the affairs of the world. Firing off emails and texts and

38. *Westminster Confession of Faith*, 21.8.
39. E.g., see Carr, *The Shallows*, 219–20.

juggling multiple chores are hardly the ideal way to prepare for worship. And when Christians observe a day and not just an hour, they also gain extended time for private worship and the opportunity to attend a second service of corporate worship, if one's church provides it, as well as time to extend and enjoy Christian hospitality.

There are other things that promote good worship when we are engaged in worship itself. In terms of private worship—both as individuals and families—minimizing distractions during times of prayer and meditation is essential if we are not to be distracted, and hence superficially engaged, during these activities. This means laying aside electronic devices. It also means finding a time and a place in which disruptions are less likely. Depending upon one's home, family, and schedule, this may not be easy, but the blessing of devoted worship makes the effort to find such times and spaces worthwhile.

In terms of corporate worship, most Christians obviously have little individual opportunity to shape its content and surroundings. But individuals can prepare themselves well for corporate worship, can train their children to behave during services, can find places to sit in the sanctuary or auditorium where distractions arise less frequently, and can certainly lay aside their phones. And those who do have authority to make decisions about the content and place of worship might remember the wisdom of the Reformed tradition in calling for unadorned meeting rooms. Although many may find a well-decorated room to be more beautiful, the minimization of distractions in an unadorned room is more likely to promote the purposes for which such a room exists: the worship of God.

The Lord's Prayer

In this chapter, I have focused upon praying and worshiping with full-hearted devotion, rather than upon the content of worship. But content *is* important, and intimately linked to internal devotion. With this in mind, I conclude this discussion with a few remarks that may help to bring the relation of the external to the internal into focus. My remarks regard the use of the Lord's Prayer as a model for our own prayers.

In Luke's gospel, Jesus teaches the Lord's Prayer in response to a request from his disciples: "Lord, teach us to pray" (Luke 11:1). This is an important fact. While we can learn many things about prayer from other prayers recorded in Scripture, this is the only one given specifically as a model and summary of godly prayer. If we wish to know what Christian prayer should look like, the Lord's Prayer is *the* place to look. As Calvin wrote, "He has given us a form in which is set before us as in a picture everything which it is lawful to wish, everything which is conducive to our interest, everything which it is necessary to demand. From his goodness in this respect we derive the great comfort of knowing, that as we ask almost in his words, we ask nothing that is absurd, or foreign, or unseasonable; nothing, in short, that is not agreeable to him."[40] If our prayers do not generally follow the pattern Christ set before us, something is amiss. This comment obviously pertains to the external form and content of prayer. Jesus taught us *what* we should pray for if we are to pray in ways pleasing to God. But this direction about form and content should also influence *how* we pray, with inward devotion of heart and mind. For one thing, it may serve as a guardrail that helps keep our minds on track and not be diverted by extraneous concerns. The Lord's Prayer does not constrain us to pray Jesus' exact words and these only, but it does provide direction, order, and purpose in our prayers that would likely elude us if God left us with complete freedom to pray, however we might feel at a given time. Furthermore, the Lord's Prayer, from its outset, provides a clue as to what is most important, and thus, what should shape the attitude of the heart through our entire prayer. What I have in mind is this: after addressing our Father in heaven, we ask that God would hallow his name. The entire Lord's Prayer unfolds as a reflection of the Christian's great desire that God's name be glorified.

The salutation of the Lord's Prayer—"Our Father, who art in heaven"—is itself remarkable. Jesus teaches us to address God with a term of intimacy and familiarity. In Jesus, we may boldly approach God as our Father and find him an all-compassionate fount of help in time of need (Heb 4:16). Addressing him as *our* Father also reminds us that we never really pray alone, by ourselves or for ourselves, even when we call out to him in total privacy. We offer our prayers alongside those of our brothers and sisters around the world, and we pray for them even as they pray for us.

Furthermore, addressing God as our Father *in heaven* presents him before our hearts as the one who dwells in triumphant glory. "In heaven" is not a geographical marker; a Christian does not refer to her divine Father in heaven in the way she may refer to her earthly father in Kansas City. The significance of God's heavenly habitation goes back to Genesis 2:1–3. God finished his creative work on earth and then took his rest in the glory of heaven. In Christ, someone in our own flesh and blood has been glorified

---

40. Calvin, *Institutes*, 3.20.34.

to God's heavenly presence and has joined him in that triumphant rest (Heb 2:5–9; 4:1–14). Those who take refuge in him have firm confidence that they already have an everlasting inheritance in that heavenly kingdom (Rom 8:14–16; Gal 4:4–7) and will one day be welcomed into that same place of glory (Heb 2:10; Rom 8:17–18). Thus, beginning our prayers by calling upon our Father in heaven should set our minds and hearts "on things above, where Christ is seated at the right hand of God" (Col 3:1). It may be a challenge to focus on a single thing with concentration and contemplation, but what a marvelous object is set before the eyes of our hearts. Surely the thought of God in his heavenly glory, where Christ even now prepares a place for us (John 14:3), should captivate his saints.

Then, after addressing God so intimately and profoundly, Christians pray: "hallowed be thy name." The very first thing we pray (in fact, the first three things we pray—half of the Lord's Prayer) is not thanksgiving or petition regarding ourselves, but a request that God do something for himself. Jesus gave us a mere six petitions in the Lord's Prayer, and the first is that God would exalt his own name.

Witsius reflects on the extraordinary privilege it is to have such intimate communion with God as prayer affords, to have Christ intercede for us, and to have the Spirit's help as we groan, but "the most wonderful of all, and one which almost exceeds belief, is that a man should be allowed to plead, not only for himself and for his neighbor, but for God,—that the kingdom of God and the glory of God should be the subject of his prayer,—as if God were unwilling to be glorious, or to exercise dominion except in answer to the prayers of believers."[41] This petition, suggests Jonathan Edwards, also indicates where our chief affections should lie: "Our last and highest end is doubtless what should be first in our *desires*, and consequently first in our *prayers*, and therefore we may argue that since Christ directs that God's glory should be first in our prayers, that therefore this is our last end."[42] Witsius is thus right to suggest that the first petition sets the tone for the rest of the prayer: "The place which this petition occupies—as *First in order*—implies a declaration, that no other object is more earnestly or cordially desired by us than the Hallowing of the Name of God. This is the ultimate end to which every thing else ought to be referred."[43] Or as

41. Witsius, *The Lord's Prayer*, 185–86.

42. Jonathan Edwards, "Concerning the End for Which God Created the World," in *Works of Jonathan Edwards*, 481. Also see John Piper, *God's Passion for His Glory*, 199.

43. Witsius, *The Lord's Prayer*, 196. See also Wilhelmus à Brakel, *The Christian's Reasonable Service*, vol. 3, trans. Bartel Elshout (Pittsburgh: Soli Deo Gloria, 1994), 3.483–84, 495, 505.

seventeenth-century Reformed theologian Wilhelmus à Brakel put it, "the five subsequent petitions are the means to that end."[44]

Conclusion

There is so much more to say about this first petition, about the Lord's Prayer as a whole, and about worship and prayer in general, but with these brief reflections on the first petition, we have come full circle in this chapter. God, above all, glorifies himself, but is pleased in part to glorify himself by glorifying us and enabling us to glorify him. The chief way God calls us to glorify him is through prayer and worship, and in a remarkably fitting way, Jesus taught us to begin our prayers by asking that God would exalt his name. In an age of distraction, when serious concentration and contemplation have become increasingly elusive, God calls us to embrace practices that promote the great privilege of worship and prayer and to resist whatever hinders them. And as we make the Lord's Prayer the great model for our own prayers, God ensures that his heavenly glory will be the first thing that meets our eyes. May it shed light on all the rest of what we pray as well, until we close by confessing that God's is "the kingdom, and the power, and the glory forever."

---

44. à Brakel, *The Christian's Reasonable Service*, 292; cf. Murray, *Principles of Conduct*, 3.507.

CHAPTER 7

The Fear of the Lord in an Age of Narcissism

"The fear of the LORD is the beginning of knowledge."
—*Proverbs 1:7*

"The fear of God in which godliness consists is the fear which consists in awe, reverence, honor, and worship."
—*John Murray*

"A narcissist is full of herself, has a big head, is a blowhard, loves the sound of his own voice, or is a legend in her own mind. . . . Narcissists are not just confident, they're overconfident. In short, narcissists admire themselves too much."
—*Jean M. Twenge and W. Keith Campbell*

A s considered at the beginning of Chapter 6, the biblical story of *soli Deo gloria* is timeless in certain respects. By his very nature God is all-glorious and worthy of all adoration. He calls human beings in all times and places to look to him and glorify him as the only true God. But in other respects, *soli Deo gloria* is time bound, for each one of us is called to glorify God in his or her own particular time and place. To honor God properly in the early twenty-first century, we must be attentive to temptations that confront us in especially strong ways. While the preceding chapter focused upon the many distractions that constantly scatter our attention, particularly during prayer and worship, this chapter ponders something even more pernicious than poor concentration: the curse of *narcissism.*

Narcissism is defined as an excessively high and unrealistic opinion about oneself and an obsession with one's public image. The terminology in the chapter title—an "age of narcissism"—might lull some readers into a premature complacency. Do we really live in an age of narcissism, and are Christians really prone to narcissistic attitudes and behavior? We may associate narcissism with extreme or even pathological conduct. The term itself, after all, derives from the character from Greek mythology, Narcissus, who looked into a pool of water and, enraptured with his own reflection, was unable to look away. Who of us is that much in love with himself? Some people also associate narcissism with a personality disorder identified by modern psychiatry. Surely, not many readers have been diagnosed as clinical narcissists.

While few readers of this book are likely to be narcissists in a clinical sense, we don't need to look too far inside our hearts to detect plenty of narcissism infecting our thoughts and desires. If many non-Christian writers see our era as an age of narcissism, how much more should Christians, alert to the deceptions of sin that plague us all, recognize the many features of our present cultural ethos that make narcissist tendencies perhaps more alluring than ever? Though I use the term "narcissism" in part for its shock value—nobody wants to be called a narcissist—I will also refer to another term, *vainglory* (or vanity), that clarifies just how implicated we all are in the kinds of sins narcissism involves. Christian moral theology has traditionally identified vainglory as one of the seven deadly vices, a vice to which every person is tempted. What modern psychology terms "narcissism" is very similar to what classical Christian theology calls "vainglory." All of us, though some more than others, become obsessed with ourselves and are blinded by desire for praise and approval by fellow human beings.

Why discuss narcissism or vainglory in a book about the Reformation motto *soli Deo gloria*? One very good reason, I believe, is because narcissism is directly contrary to one of the most fundamental marks of true godliness in Scripture, the fear of the Lord, and the fear of the Lord is essential for being a person who gives all glory to God. People can hardly fear the Lord when they're obsessed with their own images, and they can hardly render all glory to God when they do not, in holy fear, stand before him with reverence and awe. As David put it long ago, the wicked have no fear of God before their eyes, and hence flatter themselves (Ps 36:1–2). Christians, humbled by their own sinfulness and in awe of a just God who graciously gave his own Son to exalt them, are now enabled by the Spirit to view themselves rightly as they give glory to God alone.

The fear of the Lord is surely not a Christian attribute that gets enough attention today, so we will begin by considering its meaning and its rightful place in a godly moral life. Then we will reflect on narcissism and its sibling

vainglory, considering both their perennial seductions and the way contemporary life fuels their flames. Finally, we will explore how Christians,
alert to these temptations, may strive to grow in the fear of the Lord and
thus to glorify God more faithfully.

The Fear of the Lord

If you took a survey asking Christians to identify the chief attribute of
a serious believer, you'd surely get a variety of answers, but probably few
would even think to name the fear of the Lord. Yet if we did an objective
survey of Scripture, we may well conclude that the fear of the Lord is the
preeminent characteristic of the godly heart. Why does David ask for a
heart fully devoted to God? "Give me an undivided heart, that I may fear
your name" (Ps 86:11). How do we embody true wisdom? "The fear of
the LORD is the beginning of knowledge" (Prov 1:7). How does Scripture
praise Job for his piety? "This man was blameless and upright; he feared
God and shunned evil" (Job 1:1). How should we respond in light of the
great promises we have in Christ? "Let us cleanse ourselves from every
defilement of body and spirit, perfecting holiness in the fear of God" (2
Cor 7:1).[1] Based on just these few examples, we can recognize the plau-
sibility of John Murray's striking claims: "The fear of God is the soul of
godliness. . . . If we are thinking of the notes of biblical piety, none is more
characteristic than the fear of the Lord."[2]

Why is it, then, that most Christians think little about the fear of the
Lord, let alone consider it the soul of godliness? One likely reason is understandable and raises a legitimate biblical concern: Scripture speaks of God
taking away fear from those who trust in him. Who can forget the many
beautiful Old Testament promises to this effect, such as God's assurance
to Israel: "Do not fear, for I am with you; do not be dismayed, for I am
your God" (Isa 41:10). Jesus encouraged his disciples, "Do not be afraid,
little flock, for your Father has been pleased to give you the kingdom"
(Luke 12:32). Perhaps most remarkable, given the importance of love for
the Christian life, is the way John contrasts love and fear: "There is no
fear in love. But perfect love drives out fear, because fear has to do with
punishment. The one who fears is not made perfect in love" (1 John 4:18).

Another likely reason why Christians today think little about the fear

---

1. My translation.
2. John Murray, *Principles of Conduct: Aspects of Biblical Ethics* (Grand Rapids: Eerdmans,
1957), 229.

of the Lord is less noble. A proper fear of the Lord implies a high view of God and his attributes, an awe before his holiness, justice, power, wisdom, glory, and so much else. To whatever extent we humanize God and bring him down to our level—and this happens so often—the fear of the Lord will hardly make much sense to us. Thus, if we're to understand why Scripture speaks of the fear of the Lord as a mark of true believers, we need to reflect on both the different ways in which the Bible speaks of fear and on the nature of God and our relationship to him as Christians.

Reformed theologians have observed two primary ways in which Scripture speaks of "fear." On one hand, fear is characterized by terror; it is a "slavish fear," the kind that "causes a slave to do the will of his master for fear of being struck."[3] Such fear is what the psalmist captures when he muses: "Egypt was glad when they left, because dread [fear] of Israel had fallen on them" (Ps 105:38). This kind of fear is actually appropriate for those who do not belong to Christ, and hence stand under God's judgment. Having such a slavish fear of God, notes one Reformed theologian, "is better than a stubborn and insensitive despising of God and His judgments."[4] By his common grace, through which he preserves this world and human society, God has instilled a measure of this fear of God in some unbelievers, producing a dread of divine judgment that restrains them from certain evil behavior. Abimelech, king of Gerar, with whom Abraham interacted in Genesis 20–21, provides an early example in Scripture.[5] Yet what is more characteristic of unbelievers is a callous rebellion against God that refuses even to respect his awesome judgment. At the end of Paul's long catalogue of the transgressions of the wicked, Murray remarks, he locates the source of their evildoing: "There is no fear of God before their eyes" (Rom 3:18).[6]

On the other hand, Scripture speaks of a different kind of fear, a "fear of reverential awe," or a "filial fear."[7] This is a fear only Christians can experience. It expresses not terror but confidence, not self-love but love for God. "Filial fear is a holy inclination of the heart, generated by God in the hearts of his children, whereby they, out of reverence for God, take careful pains not to displease God, and earnestly endeavor to please Him in all things."[8]

---

3. à Brakel, *The Christian's Reasonable Service*, vol. 3, 233.
4. Ibid., 3.292.
5. See especially Genesis 20:11; see also the comments on this text in Murray, *Principles of Conduct*, 230; and in David VanDrunen, *Divine Covenants and Moral Order*, 157–61.
6. Murray, *Principles of Conduct*, 230–31.
7. See Murray, *Principles of Conduct*, 233; and à Brakel, *The Christian's Reasonable Service*, 3.292.
8. à Brakel, *The Christian's Reasonable Service*, 3.293 (italics in original removed).

The Christian still has, to be sure, a continuing sense of holy awe before a perfectly just and holy God who will soon bring final judgment against this world. Every godly person should shudder at the heinousness of sin and feel deep contrition before the face of an infinitely pure God.[9] But while maintaining a profound respect for the God who is coming in wrath and condemnation, Christians rejoice that they do not need to stand *personally* terrified of the coming judgment. This is one of the supreme blessings of those justified through faith in Christ: "Therefore, since we have been justified through faith, we have peace with God through our Lord Jesus Christ" (Rom 5:1), and "Since we have now been justified by his blood, how much more shall we be saved from God's wrath through him" (Rom 5:9). This so-called "filial fear" of God releases us from the "slavish fear" that rightfully held us in bondage while we languished outside of Christ. As Paul explains later in Romans, "The Spirit you received does not make you slaves, so that you live in fear again; rather, the Spirit you received brought about your adoption to sonship. And by him we cry, '*Abba*, Father'" (Rom 8:15).

The biblical texts I quoted earlier that suggest that fear is inconsistent with the Christian life refer to fearing things we need not fear as believers. We need not fear the human conqueror of earthly kingdoms (Isa 41:10; cf. Isa 41:2–7); we need not fear the loss of earthly possessions (Luke 12:32; cf. Luke 12:22–34); we need not fear punishment from God on the day of judgment (1 John 4:18; cf. 1 John 4:17). We could add to this list: we now need not fear death (Heb 2:14–15), for example, and we certainly need not fear our fellow human beings (Prov 29:25; Col 3:22).[10] These are all wonderful gifts. May Christ's words always bring us comfort: "Do not be afraid, little flock" (Luke 12:32).

Yet Christians should still have a profound filial fear of the Lord. Fearing the Lord is hardly just for sinners. Even Christ himself—the sinless Messiah—had the fear of God: "The Spirit of the LORD will rest on

---

9. Cf. Murray, *Principles of Conduct*, 235–36.

10. As à Brakel penetratingly puts it in *The Christian's Reasonable Service*: "The third sin committed against the fear of God is *to fear man*. . . . If we have not yet fully denied ourselves in regard to honor, love, advantage, and pleasure, nor are much inclined to acknowledge the insignificance of man . . . , and we have not accustomed ourselves to see the hand of the Lord in all things, thus perceiving that God alone does everything, and that all men are but instruments in His hand, being used either to do good or evil unto us—this will engender a looking unto man." "We look to men and, in our thoughts end in them—as if it had to come from them. We vehemently seek to have them on our side, and we are fearful of losing their favor" (3.299). "It is the greatest act of contempt toward God if He must yield to man for you. . . . It is a denial of the providence of God—as if God did not reign" (3.300).

him—the Spirit of wisdom and of understanding, the Spirit of counsel and of might, the Spirit of the knowledge and fear of the LORD—and he will delight in the fear of the LORD" (Isa 11:2–3). Why do Christians continue to fear God? For one thing, the very reason why we need not fear death, tyrants, or loss of earthly goods is because God is so great and powerful, and is able to protect his own from all threats of harm. In other words, the reverential awe with which we regard our God is precisely why the threats of all other foes recede from the eye of faith. Who or what could possibly stand before a God so great?

We also continue to fear God as we admire his infinitely perfect attributes that ought to "engender reverence" in us. "He is majestic, glorious, omnipotent, holy, good, and awe-inspiring."[11] Another important aspect of our fear of the Lord derives from an abiding awareness of God's presence. The foolish person is inattentive to God and forgets about him. He ignores the testimony of creation all around him (Rom 1:18–20) and the whisperings of conscience within (Rom 2:14–15). The godly Christian, on the other hand, confesses that God is present with her everywhere (Ps 139:7–10) and can say, "I keep my eyes always on the LORD" (Ps 16:8). "The first thought of the godly man in every circumstance is God's relation to him and it, and his and its relation to God. That is God-consciousness and that is what the fear of God entails."[12] In addition to these considerations, I will explain later in the chapter why Christians' filial fear is much more than simply the continuation of certain aspects of the fear of God obligatory on all people, including those outside of Christ. Our salvation in Christ, I will argue, incorporates profoundly new elements into our fear of the Lord.

Is there anything in our everyday experience that helps us to explain this reverential awe before God? The best example I can think of is the momentary wonder that can strike a person when coming face-to-face with a celebrity, especially if it's unexpected. I have had a few such experiences in my life, the most memorable being the time I stepped into the tram that runs between terminals at the Atlanta airport and suddenly found myself standing right next to one of the most famous athletes in the world, a former heavyweight boxing champion. The experience was surreal; for a few moments all other thoughts dropped from my mind and my entire attention was focused upon the fact that I was in the presence of a superstar. I had no reason to be terrified of him, but I certainly experienced a momentary sense of awe. If we can have this sort of reaction when coming

---

11. à Brakel, *The Christian's Reasonable Service*, 3.300.
12. Murray, *Principles of Conduct*, 238.

into the presence of a prominent human being, how profound will our awe be when entering the presence of the living God? If we're capable of losing ourselves in wonder at a celebrity, how much more ought we to be enraptured in our devotion before the Almighty even today?

Before we begin reflecting on the temptations of narcissism, it is worth considering specifically how the fear of the Lord is related to our larger theme of *soli Deo gloria*. As mentioned above, *reverential awe* characterizes the Christian's filial fear of God. We need not fear that he will pour out his coming wrath upon us personally, but we do regard him with the highest reverence. "The fear of God in which godliness consists," Murray writes, "is the fear which consists in awe, reverence, honor, and worship." He adds later: "The controlling sense of the majesty and holiness of God and the profound reverence which this apprehension elicits constitute the essence of the fear of God."[13] To put it simply, the reality of God's all-surpassing glory is what triggers this reverential fear of the Lord in the godly heart. Inseparable from this truth is the call to worship. Once again we perceive the centrality of prayer and worship for Christians seeking to glorify God. The glory of God spurs a reverential fear of the Lord in the godly heart, and this reverential fear cannot help but spring forth into praise. As Wilhelmus à Brakel puts it, "*Reverence* requires, first of all, a knowledge of and beholding of God's majesty. . . . Secondly, there must be a delightful acknowledgement and a wholehearted approbation that God is so majestic. . . . Thirdly, there must be a reverent bowing before the Lord and a worshiping of Him."[14]

This indeed seems to be the pattern of devotion among the saints of both the Old and New Testaments. Consider the psalmist, who describes with awe the glory of his great God: "For the LORD is the great God, the great King above all gods. In his hand are the depths of the earth, and the mountain peaks belong to him. The sea is his, for he made it, and his hands formed the dry land" (Ps 95:3–5). What is the proper response to this God? The psalmist continues, "Come, let us bow down in worship, let us kneel before the LORD our Maker" (Ps 95:6). The next psalm follows the same pattern. It begins: "Sing to the LORD a new song; sing to the LORD, all the earth. Sing to the LORD, praise his name; proclaim his salvation day after day. Declare his glory among the nations, his marvelous deeds among all peoples" (Ps 96:1–3). What motivates such worship? God's greatness, power, and glory, which engenders reverential fear in his people: "For great is the LORD and

---

13. Ibid., 236–37.
14. à Brakel, *The Christian's Reasonable Service*, 3.294.

most worthy of praise; he is to be feared above all gods. For all the gods of the nations are idols, but the LORD made the heavens. Splendor and majesty are before him; strength and glory are in his sanctuary" (Ps 96:4–6).

This pattern of devotion emerges perhaps most powerfully in all of Scripture in the final section of Hebrews 12. In light of the distinction between a slavish fear and a filial fear of the Lord, it is interesting to observe that this section begins by assuring the readers of Hebrews that they have *not* come to Mount Sinai, a place where God threatened Israel with swift and terrible judgment such that even Moses trembled with fear (Heb 12:18–21). The readers of Hebrews, including Christians today, have come instead to "Mount Zion, to the city of the living God, the heavenly Jerusalem." Through the work of Christ outlined in previous sections of Hebrews, Christians even now have communion with the angels, the glorified saints, God the Father, and his Son our savior (Heb 12:22–24). But this demands a response. We are not passive as we participate in this heavenly assembly; we are instructed: "See to it that you do not refuse him who speaks" (Heb 12:25). If God's glory was awesome on Mount Sinai, how much more glorious is he in heaven? If he shook that remote mountain in the desert long ago, how much more will he shake the whole earth when Christ returns in judgment (Heb 12:25–26)? And how wonderful it is that when he shakes the whole earth, he will establish his kingdom in all its glory, "a kingdom that cannot be shaken" (Heb 12:27–28)? What should our response be? "Let us be thankful, and so worship God acceptably with reverence and awe, for our 'God is a consuming fire'" (Heb 12:28–29). Before God's glory must be reverential awe, and this reverential awe must bring forth worship.

If Christians here and now respond to the revelation of God's glory with this worship of reverence and awe, we can only begin to imagine what our reverential worship will be like in heaven, when we will not only be free of sin but also behold the glory of Christ face to face. Our fear of the Lord will not decrease but increase. Revelation 15 offers a glimpse of the worship which the departed saints now render to God in heaven, and at its center are fear of the Lord and glorifying his name: They "sang the song of God's servant Moses and of the Lamb: 'Great and marvelous are your deeds, Lord God Almighty. Just and true are your ways, King of the nations. Who will not fear you, Lord, and bring glory to your name? For you alone are holy. All nations will come and worship before you, for your righteous acts have been revealed'" (Rev 15:3–4). Murray writes, "The fear of God is the beginning of wisdom, and the perfection of glory in the world to come will only intensify its exercise. . . . The deeper the apprehension of God's glory the more enhanced will be our wonderment. It will not be the wonderment of perplexity or horror but of reverential and exultant adoration."[15]

There is much more to say about the fear of the Lord and the corresponding virtues it supports in the godly Christian. The God-fearer exhibits humility, for example, for who can have a conceited view of himself while maintaining an exalted view of God? The God-fearer is also courageous, for who can be terrified by wicked people or other perils in this world while honoring God as ruler of all? The God-fearer also grows in wisdom, for the one who sets the Lord always before him also begins to see the world aright. We will return to some of these themes in the final section of the chapter, but first we turn to consider that great vice that stands so opposed to the fear of the Lord—narcissism—and its ugly sister, vanity.

The Seduction of Narcissism

At the beginning of this chapter, I introduced the idea of narcissism. Psychology professors Jean Twenge and Keith Campbell, who have written insightfully on narcissism in contemporary culture, describe it simply: "A narcissist is full of herself, has a big head, is a blowhard, loves the sound of his own voice, or is a legend in her own mind. . . . Narcissists are not just confident, they're overconfident. In short, narcissists admire themselves too much."[16] If that's not clear enough, they also suggest several other terms that describe facets of narcissism: "arrogance, conceit, vanity, grandiosity, and self-centeredness."[17] It's difficult to think of character traits more inimical to a healthy fear of the Lord that fosters worship with reverence and awe. The God-fearer is enraptured with the Lord; a narcissist is enraptured with himself. Being both at the same time is impossible.

Twenge and Campbell speak of a "narcissism epidemic" that has engulfed American culture, and many other cultures around the world. In the late 1970s, Christopher Lasch wrote a best-selling book entitled *The Culture of Narcissism* in which he exposed many features of American life that Twenge and Campbell argue have grown steadily since then.[18] If they're correct, it's alarming for many reasons, and Christians need

---

15. Murray, *Principles of Conduct*, 241–42.

16. Jean M. Twenge and W. Keith Campbell, *The Narcissism Epidemic: Living in the Age of Entitlement* (New York: Free Press, 2009), 18.

17. Ibid., 18.

18. Christopher Lasch, *The Culture of Narcissism: American Life in an Age of Diminishing Expectations* (New York: Norton, 1978).

to be on guard against the seductions that a narcissistic age present. But narcissism and its corresponding vices are perennial. Sinners have always been prone to think too highly of themselves. Thus, before we consider the temptations of a narcissistic age more closely, I wish to reflect briefly on one of the vices Twenge and Campbell identify as a characteristic of narcissism: vanity. Vanity is a familiar word in classical Christian moral theology—one of the seven deadly sins—and considering its character helps to put this subject in proper theological perspective.

Vanity

What exactly is vanity, or vainglory? Rebecca Konyndyk DeYoung offers this definition: "Vainglory is the excessive and disordered desire for recognition and approval from others. . . . When caught in the vice of vainglory, we want acclaim too much, so much, in fact, that we will accept it whether it is deserved or not."[19] She notes, "That the name of this vice includes the term 'glory' is apt, for this is the end those with this vice seek excessively. The vainglorious primarily desire attention, approval, and applause."[20] This observation is pertinent to our discussion, since it makes clear just how antithetical vainglory is to the theme of *soli Deo gloria*. The godly Christian seeks the glory of the Lord; the vainglorious person seeks glory for herself.

The vice of vainglory is related to several other vices, but worth distinguishing from them. Vanity and pride, for example, are close cousins. But DeYoung explains that they differ in important ways: "Pride excessively concerns excellence itself (excelling others); vainglory, by contrast, concerns primarily the *display* or manifestation of excellence." Thus, "the vainglorious . . . do not aspire to something because it is excellent. Rather, they seek whatever will bring in the most public applause, whether deserving or not."[21] This distinction clarifies why we sometimes use "pride" in a positive way. Generally, we think it is good for people to take pride in their work. It means they want to do it well. This desire for excellence only becomes a vice when it becomes excessive and disproportionate to other worthy goals. But there is no positive way to describe someone as "vainglorious." Vanity entails a desire for praise and admiration for its own

---

19. Rebecca Konyndyk DeYoung, *Glittering Vices: A New Look at the Seven Deadly Sins and Their Remedies* (Grand Rapids: Brazos, 2009), 60. Since I completed writing this book DeYoung has published another work on vice devoted especially to vanity; see Rebecca Konyndyk DeYoung, *Vainglory: The Forgotten Vice* (Grand Rapids: Eerdmans, 2014).

20. Ibid., 63.

21. Ibid., 62.

sake, unhinged from the excellence of one's character or work—that is, unhinged from whether or not such praise is deserved. "For the vainglorious," DeYoung writes, "image is everything."[22]

We can see the total incongruity between the obsession with self-image on the part of the vainglorious person and the God-fearing person who says with the psalmist, "Not to us, LORD, not to us but to your name be the glory" (Ps 115:1). We can also see that vanity inevitably involves a disregard for the truth. However many attributes or accomplishments a person has that may rightfully deserve some praise, there are also bound to be so many flaws and failures that the vainglorious person has to engage in a campaign of deception in order to keep the truth about him from getting out. Hence hypocrisy, one of the most reviled vices, "is the natural result of a heart sold out to vainglory."[23]

A Culture of Narcissism

Vainglory, thus understood, is a vice against which Christians of every historical age must be on guard. But here is a good point to return to our discussion of narcissism and the idea that we live today in a culture of narcissism, or even in the midst of a narcissism epidemic: if the above is true, we need to be on special guard against this vice. And the evidence that ours is indeed an age of narcissism is, unfortunately, quite compelling.

Although Lasch utilized a great deal of Freudian analysis in his study of narcissism in America, some of the colloquial ways he describes narcissism will sound familiar after reflecting on the vice of vainglory. The narcissist, for example, is "fiercely competitive in his demand for approval and acclaim." "Notwithstanding his occasional illusions of omnipotence, the narcissist depends on others to validate his self-esteem. He cannot live without an admiring audience."[24] Among other narcissistic traits Lasch also mentions acquisitiveness, "in the sense that his cravings have no limits" and a chronic boredom "restlessly in search of instantaneous intimacy."[25]

Despite the Freudian and Marxist elements of Lasch's study, as well as the lapse of time since its publication, many claims about his own cultural ethos still seem true today—maybe even more so. He speaks, for example, of a dread of old age that hits even before the onset of middle age. The narcissist needs admiration for things such as beauty, charm, and power,

22. Ibid., 63.
23. Ibid., 69.
24. Lasch, *The Culture of Narcissism*, xvi, 10.
25. Ibid., xvi, 40.

things that tend to fade over time, and thus, he desires to preserve his youth.[26] Lasch also speaks of how parents breed narcissistic personality traits in their children by trying to give them the favored position in the family, and he finds something analogous in schools, where teachers follow "the line of least resistance . . . by making the experience as painless as possible. Hoping to avoid confrontations and quarrels, they leave the students without guidance, meanwhile treating them as if they were incapable of serious exertion."[27] Lasch also traces a shift from seeking others' esteem through one's accomplishments to a craving for admiration based on personal attributes. Rather than desiring respect, people want to be envied; they have moved from pride to vanity.[28] Success, he says, needs to be ratified by publicity, and "impressions overshadow achievements."[29] "Advertising," furthermore, "serves not so much to advertise products as to promote consumption as a way of life."[30] When reading many of these descriptions, we may want to move back in time and tell Lasch, as he is writing in the 1970s, *you should see things now*!

The Narcissism Epidemic

Twenge and Campbell are observing culture today as well as referencing the past, and they identify the 1970s as the beginning of what has become a full-scale narcissism epidemic.[31] Early in their study, they identify some misconceptions about narcissism. Perhaps most importantly, they argue that narcissism is *not* a product of low self-esteem. Many people assume that narcissistic behavior stems from hating oneself, but to the contrary, Twenge and Campbell demonstrate, "deep down inside, narcissists think they're *awesome*."[32] They don't hate themselves, but are instead madly in love with themselves. Misconceiving narcissists as self-haters means that people also get the cure for narcissism wrong. When a teenage girl posts revealing pictures of herself online, her parents tell her all the more adamantly how special and beautiful she is. "This is like suggesting an obese person would feel much better if she just ate more doughnuts," write Twenge and Campbell. "Megan wants everyone to see just how beautiful and special she is, and it's not because she thinks she is ugly—it's because

26. Ibid., 41, 210.
27. Ibid., 50, 140.
28. Ibid., 59.
29. Ibid., 60.
30. Ibid., 72.
31. Twenge and Campbell, *The Narcissism Epidemic*, 68.
32. Ibid., 24–28.

she thinks she's hot."[33] Narcissism, in other words, resembles the vain-glory we considered above. The narcissist is obsessed with her own image, even at the inevitable expense of truth. This is because narcissists, Twenge and Campbell point out, are not in reality any greater, better looking, or smarter than other people.[34]

If narcissism, vainglory, and related vices are perennial plagues of sinful humanity, what is the evidence that narcissism has reached epidemic propor-tions in contemporary American society (and increasingly elsewhere, too)? Initially, Twenge and Campbell point to studies showing that, by 2006, "1 out of 4 college students agreed with the majority of the items on a standard measure of narcissistic traits," and that almost 1 out of 10 Americans in their twenties have experienced symptoms of the clinically diagnosed Narcissistic Personality Disorder. "Lurking underneath," Twenge and Campbell assert, "is the narcissistic culture that has drawn in many more."[35]

One prime instigator of the current epidemic they point to takes us back to our high-tech Internet culture and especially social networking. While Twenge and Campbell see the 1970s as the advent of the epidemic, they wonder aloud whether 2005–06, with the emergence of Facebook and YouTube, may turn out "to be a second inflection point for the growth of the narcissism epidemic."[36] Twenge and Campbell hardly come across as technology haters, but observe that "social networking sites shape the ways teens and twentysomethings view their worlds, and mold the mal-leable personality of young people like clay. Just as animals evolve and change to fit into their environments, young people are becoming more narcissistic to fit into the demands of the new digital world."[37] Twenge and Campbell point to four key messages that social networking culture instills in people—especially young people: the need for constant entertainment, flaunt it if you've got it, success through being a consumer, and attaining happiness through glamorous adulthood (the latter primarily understood in a sexual context). "All of these messages are consistent with a growing culture of narcissism, with its rampant materialism, aggression toward oth-ers, vanity, shallow sexuality, and rabid desire for attention and fame."[38] They add, furthermore, that "the structure of the sites rewards the skills

---

33. Ibid., 8–9.
34. Ibid., 28.
35. Ibid., 2.
36. Ibid., 69.
37. Ibid., 114.
38. Twenge and Campbell, *The Narcissism Epidemic*, 108. They derive these four points from Candice M. Kelsey, *Generation MySpace: Helping Your Teen Survive Online Adolescence* (New York: Marlowe, 2007).

of the narcissist, such as self-promotion, selecting flattering photographs of oneself, and having the most friends."[39]

We don't have to deny the legitimate uses of social networking to recognize the need for vigilance in using the forms of media that are so often means of promoting vices that undermine the fear of the Lord. Christians must recognize their own vulnerability to sin and the special attractions of vanity. In many respects the temptations are not new, but their opportunities to seduce us seem to be greater than ever. As DeYoung notes, regarding how vainglory tends to spawn boastfulness: "YouTube and other Internet sites like it are just the newest venues for displaying this ancient vice and creating publicity for one's achievements."[40]

Twenge and Campbell cite many other pieces of evidence beyond the Internet and social networking culture to establish their claim of a narcissism epidemic. They pay special attention, for example, to the boom in easy credit that came to a head in the financial crisis of 2008–09. Easy credit means people are able to buy more things—things they wouldn't otherwise be able to purchase and which, in any case, they really cannot afford. The personal temptation to buy on credit beyond one's means is only heightened when one's friends and neighbors take the bait and create pressure to keep up. "Rather than earning wealth, people today can borrow it and simply pretend to themselves and others that they have made it. Narcissism is linked to this quest for material goods and a 'beat the Joneses' lifestyle. For narcissists, material goods such as a Rolex watch, a luxury car, and a huge kitchen with granite countertops are signals of status."[41]

In the years following the financial crisis in America, the opportunities to avail oneself of easy credit have lessened somewhat for purchasing certain items, but the temptations are still everywhere, and at the time I write this, the levels of household debt in America seem to have ceased their several-year decline. Artificially low (non-market-based) interest rates imposed by the Federal Reserve for an extended period of time were one of the chief causes of the financial crisis, and now, ironically, even lower interest rates for an even longer period of time have become its chief means for trying to counter the financial crisis. Central banks impose artificially low interest rates for one basic reason: to encourage borrowing—and hence spending—beyond what ordinary market conditions suggest is reasonable.[42] There

---

39. Twenge and Campbell, *The Narcissism Epidemic*, 110.
40. DeYoung, *Glittering Vices*, 70.
41. Twenge and Campbell, *The Narcissism Epidemic*, 129.
42. They do also impose them to encourage investment in riskier assets, such as equities and real estate. But it amounts to the same thing.

remains plenty of borrowing opportunity—far too much opportunity—for the narcissist to resist.

Twenge and Campbell highlight several other symptoms and stimulants of the narcissism epidemic that I will note more briefly. They point, for example, to the rather staggering figure that cosmetic surgery in the United States increased *five times* between 1997 and 2007.[43] They discuss how fewer and fewer parents give their children ordinary names and more and more give them unusual and eccentric names—trying hard to make each of their children special.[44] On the subject of children's specialness, Twenge and Campbell also note that "I am a special person" is one of the items appearing on the Narcissistic Personality Inventory, yet this is now a message that parents and teachers feel they must instill in the young. Twenge and Campbell counter, "Feeling special is narcissism—not self-esteem, not self-confidence, and not something we should be building in our children."[45] A final item worth mentioning is these authors' discussion of *entitlement*, "the pervasive belief that one deserves special treatment, success, and more material things. Entitlement is one of the key components of narcissism, and one of the most damaging to others."[46] They chronicle the increased need for praise and the diminished drive to work hard that characterizes so many students and (especially younger) workers today—as many teachers and employers can readily testify.[47]

Fostering the Fear of the Lord, for His Glory

Reflecting on the vice of vainglory is a sobering exercise, and adding our culture of narcissism to the mix is more sobering still. As sinful creatures, we're prone to seek our own glory rather than God's, to be enamored with ourselves rather than him, and our present cultural ethos provides this evil inclination with plenty of encouragement. Yet we are called to glorify God and, as we have considered, we cannot glorify God without a robust reverence and awe for him. How can we cultivate a healthy fear of the Lord and thereby counter the pernicious allure of narcissism?

The discussion of narcissism in the previous section suggests several practical considerations that may diminish temptations to vanity and wean us away from narcissistic patterns of conduct. Some Christians may find

---

43. Twenge and Campbell, *The Narcissism Epidemic*, 148.
44. Ibid., 180.
45. Ibid., 189, 191.
46. Ibid., 230.
47. Ibid., chap. 14.

it necessary to modify their use of social media in order to break the habits of self-promotion these media forms often foster. Others may need to cut themselves off from the various lines of credit that encourage living beyond one's means and trying to bolster one's status before neighbors and co-workers. Many Christians certainly need to examine the messages they send to their impressionable children, both by explicit instruction and by subtle example. We must try to counter the misleading cultural messages about self-esteem, specialness, and entitlement, and instead help our children to evaluate themselves honestly before God and to learn industriousness and gratitude—but we are likely to fail if our conduct does not match our rhetoric.

In this final section of the chapter, however, I wish to focus not on these important practical concerns but upon some wonderful theological truths. These truths should help us maintain proper perspective with respect to ourselves, to God, and to our relationship with him. And it is not as if these theological truths are impractical. On the contrary, it is only with the perspective these truths provide that any efforts against narcissism and toward the fear of the Lord can expect success.

I believe a fitting place to begin is with a point simultaneously theological and ethical: we must be people who love the *truth*, both about God and ourselves. Narcissism preys upon self-deception. To be a narcissist requires an unrealistic and exaggerated sense of one's own worth, an inaccurate assessment of one's abilities, accomplishments, good looks, or popularity. And falsely assessing ourselves necessarily infects our assessment of God. How can we recover a proper assessment of God and ourselves over and against the internal and external seductions of vainglory?

A proper self-assessment depends greatly on the virtue of humility. For example, Twenge and Campbell write: "In many ways, humility is the opposite of narcissism." Why is this? While narcissism involves self-deception, "true humility is . . . the ability to see or evaluate yourself accurately and without defensiveness."[48] Humility does not mean that we can't recognize where our strengths and abilities lie. Such insight is necessary to make wise decisions about life. So-called "false humility" is just that—*false*. But when we examine ourselves truthfully, our Christian doctrine of sin assures us that we will find much to be humble about. Our greatest strengths, our most admirable achievements, our most winning attributes—evil desires and sinful shortcomings intermix with them all.

---

48. Ibid., 282, 283.

Even our best works are as dirty rags (Isa 64:6). And even that which is truly righteous about our good works, we acknowledge, are simply the product of God's grace at work in us, and thus certainly not matters for boasting. It is not as if humility is appropriate only for certain wicked and untalented people when they're honest about themselves. Humility is fitting for every last sinner who assesses himself properly.

Even more important is our need to embrace the truth about God. If we measure ourselves according to a standard of our own creation, or even on a curve in comparison with other human beings, we may well find things in ourselves to boast about. But the true source of godly humility comes in recognizing that we stand always before the living God. When we recognize his greatness, his holiness, his wisdom, and all his infinite attributes, we finally see ourselves for what we truly are. Acknowledging God's attributes does not strip away narcissism simply by disabusing us of our pretenses to greatness; however, it builds in us the fear of God that we seek as foundation for glorifying him in all we do. The Westminster Shorter Catechism (Answer 4) states that "God is a Spirit, infinite, eternal, and unchangeable, in his being, wisdom, power, holiness, justice, goodness, and truth." Memorizing this would be good for our minds, but digesting its message ought to strike our hearts. God is infinite, eternal, and unchangeable in his being. God is infinite, eternal, and unchangeable in his wisdom. God is infinite, eternal, and unchangeable in his power. And he is thus in all his other attributes. This is literally incomprehensible. How can such a God not elicit reverence and awe? How can we not fear such a God? How could such a God not be worthy of all glory? Being a vainglorious narcissist before the face of this God is absurd, ridiculous, and bizarre.

The Gospel and Christian Humility

But even with all of this discussion, we still have not dug quite deeply enough. We need to consider how the gospel of Jesus Christ shapes our view of God, hence our fear of God, and thus, the call to humility as we stand before him. Clearly, the fear of God is not just the responsibility of believers saved through Christ. We have already considered how all human beings are bound to fear God and have plenty of reasons to do so even in light of what we know about him from natural revelation. Those who have come to faith in Christ continue to have these reasons for fearing God, though we are so thankful that we need not be personally terrified of his coming judgment. But an issue we haven't yet discussed is whether *the gospel itself*—and by this I mean the message and blessings of salvation in Christ—also enriches and transforms this fear of God that obligates all human beings. It does indeed, I believe, and therefore also enriches and transforms our practice of humility. This is surely worthy of a lengthier discussion, but I offer here a couple of considerations that I hope will encourage further reflection.

A biblical text that seems to make the point as clearly as any is Psalm 130:3–4: "If you, O Lord, kept a record of sins, O Lord, who could stand? But with you there is forgiveness; therefore you are feared." The basic movement of thought is easy to see. If the just and holy God held our sins against us, not a single person could endure his judgment. But he is also a God of forgiveness, which means that his saints can indeed stand before him. And *because of this*, we fear him.

The way this English translation puts it suggests that God's forgiveness of sins, which lies at the heart of the gospel, is the cause (or at least *a* cause) of our fear of the Lord. The Hebrew text of Psalm 130:4 actually suggests a slightly different reading, although it conveys a similar theological point. It says that with God there is forgiveness, *in order that* he may be feared. God forgives us for the very purpose of stirring us to fear him. The King James Version reflects this reading: "But *there is* forgiveness with thee, that thou mayest be feared." At first glance, it seems almost as though we have no reason to fear God apart from his forgiving us. We know this is not true, but it must then be the case that there is some aspect of the fear of the Lord that we cannot grasp and practice until we have experienced his forgiving grace in Christ. What aspect is it?

I suggest that it's the reverence and awe that springs from our comprehension of God's saving mercy. It is interesting that Answer 4 of the Westminster Shorter Catechism lists many awe-inspiring attributes of God but does not mention his saving grace. (His saving grace is an aspect of his goodness, which it does mention, but there is much more to his goodness than just his grace.) What the Shorter Catechism does is list divine attributes knowable to everyone, everywhere. All people, even through natural revelation, know something of God's being, wisdom, power, holiness, justice, goodness, and truth. But what all people do not necessarily know—and to be more precise, what all people who have not heard the gospel of Christ do *not* know—is that God forgives sin through the life, death, and resurrection of his Son.

But to know this surely enriches and transforms our view of God. A

God who is infinitely just, holy, and powerful surely deserves our awe. But is our awe for him not magnified by knowing that this perfectly holy and just God actually *forgives sins*? This God who has said that he will *not* justify the wicked (Exod 23:7), and indeed that justifying the guilty is an abomination to him (Prov 17:15), now comes to us in the gospel and reveals himself as the God who "justifies the ungodly" (Rom 4:5). Furthermore, we learn in the gospel that in doing so, God does not in the least compromise his justice, holiness, truth, or any other of his attributes, for he has sent his own Son in the likeness of sinful flesh (Rom 8:3), and he "bore our sins in his body on the cross" (1 Pet 2:24). "It was not with perishable things such as silver or gold that you were redeemed . . . but with the precious blood of Christ, a lamb without blemish or defect" (1 Pet 1:18–19). Christ has also been obedient in our place (Rom 5:19), and God imputes his righteousness to us (Rom 4:6, 11). Who cannot stand in awe of a God whose love is so deep, so profound, so generous? How can Christians not fear the Lord so much more richly than unbelievers ever could?

On this note, it is also appropriate to return to a text considered earlier: Hebrew 12:18–29. Since these verses specifically address Christians—who even now participate in the worship of the heavenly Mount Zion—and conclude by exhorting them to worship God with reverence and awe, we must wonder again if there is something about Christians' experience of the gospel that enriches and transforms their fear of the Lord. Some aspects of this text present God in ways that all people know, and indeed ways that all people will eventually experience. I think specifically of how it describes God as a God of judgment and wrath, revealed long ago at Mount Sinai (12:18–21) and to be revealed most terrifyingly at the judgment of the last day (12:26–27). Christians may certainly not forget that he is such a God. This text even warns them, "See to it that you do not refuse him who speaks. If they did not escape when they refused him who warned them on earth, how much less will we, if we turn away from him who warns us from heaven" (12:25)? Yet this warning is not what immediately precedes and grounds the exhortation to worship God with reverence and awe; what precedes and grounds it is a command to be grateful for "receiving a kingdom that cannot be shaken" (12:28). That God comes in judgment against sin is awe-inspiring indeed. But that God would give to rebellious sinners an unshakable kingdom even while he shakes and removes all else (12:26–27)—now that should inspire awe like nothing else we could ever imagine.

This deepening of the fear of God through the gospel surely ought also to deepen our humility. By this, I mean not that the gospel should humble us further by debasing us, but that it should make us more profoundly honest about ourselves and help us understand more exactly what our true worth is before God. For one thing, the gospel message serves to bring our sinfulness into stark relief. It does so in several ways, but perhaps most profoundly by displaying that our sin is so heinous before the sight of a just and holy God that it took *the death of God's own Son* to save us. If any doubt lingers about just how lost we were in our sins, this fact should expunge it forever.

Another way in which the gospel deepens our humility is by keeping it from turning into utter despair. Despair would seem to be the only logical response if *all* we knew about ourselves was our sinfulness and consequent condemnation before God's judgment. But humility grounded in the gospel enables us to understand that we do have true worth and that we are, in fact, called to glory. It is not a worth that derives from our own efforts and not a glory we can achieve by our own strength. Rather, the gospel reveals our worth as those renewed in the image of God through Christ, empowers us to do works that are truly good and honorable,[49] and gives us hope of a coming glory bestowed by Christ at his second coming. As we considered in earlier chapters, the fact that all glory belongs to God *alone* and that we, too, will be glorified on the last day is no contradiction. God glorifies himself in all his works, but is especially pleased to glorify himself through the glorification of his saints in Christ—whose very glorification thus redounds back to the glory of God. The idea of a humble glorification seems oxymoronic. But insofar as our glorification serves God's greater glory, it begins to make wonderful sense.

May we who trust in Christ give all glory to God as we fear him in humble reverence. May we fear him humbly in light of all of his attributes and works. But may we fear and glorify him especially for doing precisely what it took, at such great cost to himself, to redeem lowly sinners and make us glorified citizens of a kingdom that can never be shaken.

---

49. DeYoung's comments on the virtue of magnanimity may be appropriate here: "Magnanimous people concern themselves with achieving great and hard-won acts of virtue as something to which God has called them. Their achievements are genuinely worthy of honor. They are things that turn our thoughts to the glory of God because they obviously aren't something anyone could have done without grace. Magnanimous people radiate God's beauty and goodness in the world, drawing others to that glory. . . ." See *Glittering Vices*, 65.

CHAPTER 8

Glorifying God in an Age That Is Passing

"They that wait upon the LORD shall renew their strength; they shall mount up with wings as eagles; they shall run, and not be weary; and they shall walk, and not faint."
—*Isaiah 40:31, KJV*

"We have a frenzied desire, an infinite eagerness, to pursue wealth and honor, intrigue for power, accumulate riches, and collect all those frivolities which seem conducive to luxury and splendor." —*John Calvin*

This book has attempted to describe Scripture's teaching about the glory of God, following the helpful lead of the Protestant Reformers and early Reformed theology. Glory is one of God's attributes—this fact grounds the conviction that all glory belongs to God alone: *soli Deo gloria*. Glory is one of the characteristics that makes God who he is, and all of his characteristics are glorious. Scripture also teaches that God reveals his glory in the very structure of the world he has made and in all the works he performs. God manifested his glory in a unique way to Israel in the pillar of cloud and fire in the wilderness, and this pillar came to rest upon the tabernacle and later the temple in Jerusalem, marking the place where God was especially pleased to dwell with his people. Yet God's sinful people constantly showed themselves unworthy of his holy presence. Thus, his glory eventually departed from their temple, and he expelled them from the Promised Land into exile in Babylon.

After many years, God graciously restored his people from exile and promised them a greater and enduring revelation of his glory in the future. This promise came to fulfillment in the coming of the Lord Jesus Christ— the Son of God incarnate—whose glory was largely veiled during his earthly ministry, but whom God raised to life and seated at his right hand in the glory of heaven. This story of God's glory will come to spectacular and everlasting conclusion on the great day when the Lord Jesus returns, revealing the new heavens and new earth and welcoming us, his perfected people, into that state of unending glory.

As we've also considered, interpreting *soli Deo gloria* along these lines is different from how it is often portrayed today. Many people speak of *soli Deo gloria* as if its main point concerns our own activity, that is, glorifying God by faithful activity that has a transformative impact on the surrounding culture. I hope the discussion of Reformation and early Reformed thought on this subject, and especially the extended study of biblical teaching, will help to enrich the church's understanding of the great theme of *soli Deo gloria* and encourage a shift in emphasis in how it's presented.

But Scripture does speak clearly of Christians glorifying God. We have seen that one of the ways God glorifies himself is by saving a people for himself. He enables them to glorify him primarily through their worship, and secondarily through all of their holy conduct, and he will one day glorify himself through glorifying his saints, granting them everlasting communion with Christ in the glory of the new creation. But it is helpful to remember that the idea of Christians glorifying God in all their life activities is not the primary way in which Scripture speaks of God's glory, and when Scripture does speak about this, it never associates it with a program of cultural transformation (though we trust that God will use our godly conduct to bless those around us).

Related to these considerations is a curiosity and a challenge that I wish to take up in this final chapter: Scripture calls us to glorify God here and now in this present age, but simultaneously speaks of this present age as *not* an age of glory. In contrast to the glorious age to come, this present age is one of suffering, sorrow, and decay. In the midst of this age, and without changing its nature, God calls believers to glorify him as they hope earnestly and wait eagerly for the dawn of the age to come. As Christ's glory was manifest, yet so largely hidden under the ugliness and brutality of his suffering unto death, so Christ's heavenly glory is already being manifest in us, but only in a way that is veiled through the sufferings, disappointments, and persecutions of this world.

Thus the questions with which this book concludes concern the nature of this present age—an age *not* of glory—and the God-glorifying way of life appropriate for those living in such an age. In the previous two chapters, I used the term "age" colloquially, to speak of early twenty-first-century culture: an "age" of distraction and narcissism. In this chapter I use the term in a common biblical sense. The "age that is passing," as the chapter title puts it, refers to the entire period in which the New Testament church has lived; in fact, it could even refer to the entire period between the fall of Adam and the second coming of Christ. The life God calls us to live in such an age, we will see, is one of grateful service yet also eager expectation, one of industrious activity yet also patient waiting. As God was glorified in Christ's humiliation and apparent defeat, so he is glorified in our patient yet joyful endurance through much suffering and humiliation.

This Present Evil Age

In this first section we consider the nature of this present age, which should be helpful background for reflecting later in the chapter upon the kind of faithful, God-glorifying life we are called to live in the midst of it. We will see here that this present age, at heart, is "evil" (Gal 1:4). It is not an age of glory. Yet God, in his providential mercy, continues to uphold this world and to preserve many good things that his hands have made. It is precisely within this age that God builds his church and sanctifies Christians to his holy service.

A number of New Testament books use the term "age" in the way I do here, but "age" is especially important in the epistles of Paul. In fact, the idea that there are *two ages* is crucial for understanding Paul's thought. In most places where he uses this terminology, he refers to either one age or the other, but both ages are mentioned in Ephesians 1:21, where Paul speaks of the resurrected Christ being seated at God's right hand above every power, "not only in the present age but also in the one to come." For Paul, this present age is the world as it lies infected by sin under the curse of God, while the age to come is the heavenly new creation in which the saints will dwell with the Lord forever in glory. God sent his Son "to rescue us from the present evil age" (Gal 1:4) and has already lavished many blessings of that coming age upon us, but Christians still live within the confines of the present age and still struggle with sin and languish under the curse. Thus, we may say that Christians live in the overlap of the two ages during their earthly life.[1]

Although Paul speaks a great deal about the heavenly new creation, when he uses the terminology of "age," he usually refers to the present age.

---

1.   This idea is illustrated in Geerhardus Vos, *The Pauline Eschatology* (Grand Rapids: Eerdmans, 1972), 38.

In addition to describing it as "evil" (Gal 1:4), he writes of the "philosopher of this age" (1 Cor 1:20) and the "wisdom of this age" (1 Cor 2:6), which are actually foolish. The "rulers of this age" (1 Cor 2:6, 8) do not understand divine wisdom and will come to nothing. Hence, Christians should not think of themselves as wise "by the standards of this age" (1 Cor 3:18). Elsewhere Paul speaks of "the god of this age"—probably Satan—who blinds unbelievers and makes them unable to see the glory of God in Christ (2 Cor 4:4). In the midst of "this present age" Christians need to learn to refuse ungodliness and worldly passions (Titus 2:12). The picture here is decidedly negative. This present age is one of vanity and presents dangers and temptations that Christians must shun. Believers ought to "lay up treasure for themselves as a firm foundation for the coming age, so that they may take hold of the life that is truly life" (1 Tim 6:19). The coming age is indeed one of "eternal life," as Jesus put it (Mark 10:18; Luke 18:30).

Another way to view the contrast between the two ages is in terms of *glory*, our chief subject. Paul speaks of this present age in contrast to the glory of the age to come. For example, the "god of this age" blinds unbelievers' minds, "so that they cannot see the light of the gospel that displays the glory of Christ, who is the image of God" (2 Cor 4:4). The darkness of this age seeks to obscure the light and glory of Christ. In the surrounding context, Paul emphasizes that believers have "the light of the knowledge of God's glory displayed in the face of Christ (2 Cor 4:6), and are being transformed into Christ's image from glory unto glory (2 Cor 3:18), but as they live in this world, such glory is muted and veiled. Paul says that he and his colleagues "have this treasure in jars of clay" (2 Cor 4:7). They are hard pressed, perplexed, persecuted, and struck down; they carry the death of Jesus in their own bodies (2 Cor 4:8–10). Paul's hope of deliverance from this state is nothing short of the resurrection (2 Cor 4:14). He ends this discussion by contrasting their participation in the decay of the present world with the glory of the age to come: "Though outwardly we are wasting away, yet inwardly we are being renewed day by day. For our light and momentary troubles are achieving for us an eternal glory that far outweighs them all. So we fix our eyes not on what is seen, but on what is unseen, since what is seen is temporary, but what is unseen is eternal" (2 Cor 4:16–18). Although Paul does not use the "age" terminology in Romans 8:17–18, he makes a similar point there: "Now if we are children, then we are heirs—heirs of God and co-heirs with Christ, if indeed we share in his sufferings in order that we may also share in his glory."

This Pauline language of two "ages" is very important, yet in and of itself insufficient for a full understanding of the present world and our place within it. When Paul speaks explicitly of this present "age" in the examples above, he speaks of it in entirely negative terms. This present age, for Paul, is evil, deceived, and opposed to the gospel. But Scripture also makes clear that this world in which we live is not entirely and unambiguously evil. God created this world, and his glory still shines within it (Ps 19:1). He satisfies the desires of every living thing (Ps 145:16), giving sun and rain to all people (Matt 5:45) and providing them crops, foods, and joy (Acts 14:17). He establishes civil magistrates to do justice for our good (Rom 13:1–4). Therefore, Paul uses "this age" to describe the world insofar as it is evil and in rebellion against God, but there are other ways to describe the world that capture these positive things—these divine blessings—that still exist around us.

The Reformation Idea of "Two Kingdoms"

The Reformation idea of the "two kingdoms" can be very helpful here. This "two kingdoms" distinction is similar in certain respects to the "two ages" distinction, but is best seen as a complement to it. In other words, both the two ages and the two kingdoms describe biblical truths about this world and the world to come, but they do not describe exactly the same truths. To get a more complete biblical picture, we need to understand both distinctions.

Here is a brief way to understand the difference between the "two ages" and the "two kingdoms": On one hand, the "two ages" refers to this present age insofar as it is cursed and in rebellion against God and to the age to come as the glory of the new heaven and new earth. This age lies under the tyranny and deception of Satan, while the age to come displays the triumph and glory of God in Christ. The "two kingdoms," on the other hand, refer to a "civil" or "common" kingdom by which God upholds the activities and institutions of this world despite its fall into sin and to a "spiritual" or "redemptive" kingdom by which God saves a people for himself, gathering them now into the church and one day bringing them home to the new creation. God is therefore the king of both kingdoms, although he rules them by different means and for different purposes.[2]

---

2. For further explanation and defense of this two kingdoms doctrine, see David VanDrunen, *Living in God's Two Kingdoms: A Biblical Vision for Christianity and Culture* (Wheaton, IL: Crossway, 2010).

A biblical text that elucidates God's rule over the common kingdom is Genesis 8:21–9:17, which describes the covenant he makes with Noah after the great flood. God establishes this covenant with *all* living creatures (Gen 9:12, 15–16), and even the entire created order (Gen 8:22; 9:13). He promises the preservation of this present world, not salvation through the forgiveness of sins or everlasting life. He vows never to destroy the earth again with a flood (Gen 8:21; 9:15), but to maintain seasons and years (Gen 8:20), the boundaries between humans and animals (Gen 9:2), human procreation (Gen 9:1, 7), and civil justice (Gen 9:6). He will do this for as long as the earth endures (Gen 8:20). This world God preserves, the common kingdom, is obviously fallen and sinful, yet God sustains much good within it. It is a kingdom of common grace,[3] which refers to "every favour of whatever kind or degree, falling short of salvation, which this undeserving and sin-cursed world enjoys at the hand of God," as John Murray put it.[4]

Thus, while we describe the world in this "present age" as cursed and hostile to God, we can also appreciate the manifold blessings still present within it, insofar as we see God's providential hand at work through the "common kingdom." There is much darkness and opposition to the gospel around us, but at most times and in most places, the world is still livable for us. Christians can ordinarily survive in their societies and lead productive lives, though the degree to which they can freely worship and evangelize differs greatly from place to place.

The way Scripture speaks about the "kingdom of heaven" or "kingdom of God"—the other of the "two kingdoms"—bears many similarities to the biblical "age to come." In Scripture this kingdom of God is ultimately a heavenly kingdom to be fully manifested in the coming new creation, yet God provided a glimpse of it in the coming of his Son and continues to do so through the life and ministry of Christ's church.[5] Many adjectives are fitting to describe this kingdom. It is a "spiritual" kingdom in that it is not an appendage to civil government or any other social institution of this world; it is a "redemptive" kingdom in that it bestows salvation from sins and everlasting life on its citizens. The Westminster Confession of Faith identifies this kingdom with the church, insofar as the kingdom is

---

3.   Among many other theologians treating this covenant with Noah as a common grace covenant, see Abraham Kuyper, *Common Grace*, vol 1.1, trans. Nelson D. Kloosterman and Ed M. van der Maas (Grand Rapids: Christian's Library Press, 2013), 15–117.

4.   John Murray, *Collected Writings*, vol. 2 (Carlisle, PA: Banner of Truth, 1977), 96.

5.   For defense of this, see VanDrunen, *Living in God's Two Kingdoms*, chap. 5.

revealed here and now.[6] The Westminster Shorter Catechism adds more detail, speaking of this kingdom as the "kingdom of grace" that advances through the church in this world and as the "kingdom of glory" that will be fully displayed and enjoyed at Christ's second coming.[7] Indeed, the kingdom *as the fully manifested new creation in the age to come* is the "kingdom of glory." Glory awaits, but for now, God's glory is largely veiled in a perishing, though preserved, world.

These theological concepts of "two ages" and "two kingdoms" provide a useful perspective for understanding the present world, particularly in comparison to the coming new creation. But what is the Christian's basic position in this world? What is the Christian's status? Three biblical ideas help to answer these questions and thus, to set the stage for our consideration, in the next section, of some specific ways in which God calls Christians to live in this present age. These three ideas are *sojourning*, *exile*, and *dual citizenship*.

Sojourning, Exile, and Dual Citizenship

First, the New Testament refers to us as *sojourners* in this world. Peter calls us to conduct ourselves in reverent fear during the time of our sojourning (1 Pet 1:17), and says that as sojourners we should abstain from sinful desires (1 Pet 2:11). Some English translations use words other than "sojourning" and "sojourners" to translate the Greek terms Peter used, but what's important is that Peter's terms refer to people living or traveling through a place that is not their true home. This is what characterizes the Christian life here in this world. The Christian's true home is Christ's heavenly kingdom, as Peter taught earlier in his first epistle: God "has given us new birth into a living hope through the resurrection of Jesus Christ from the dead, and into an inheritance that can never perish, spoil or fade. This inheritance is kept in heaven for you" (1 Pet 1:3–4).

The idea of pilgrimage would have been familiar to Peter's readers who knew the Old Testament. Genesis describes Abraham as a sojourner on many occasions (Gen 12:10; 15:13; 20:1; 21:34; 23:4). In fact, the Greek translation of the Old Testament (the "Septuagint"), which many original readers of 1 Peter would have known, uses the same Greek words to describe Abraham that Peter uses to describe Christians. After God called him out of Ur of the Chaldeans, Abraham never settled anywhere for very long. He

---

6. *Westminster Confession of Faith*, 25.2.
7. *Westminster Shorter Catechism*, 102.

moved about from place to place. But as Hebrews explains, Abraham was not a sojourner simply because he had multiple homes on earth. He was a sojourner on earth because his permanent home was in heaven: Abraham was "looking forward to the city with foundations, whose architect and builder is God" (Heb 11:10), and was "longing for a better country—a heavenly one" (Heb 11:16). So it is with Christians today. A particular Christian may spend her whole earthly life living in one place, but she is still a sojourner on earth because she is away from her heavenly homeland. Even a seemingly settled life in this world is, in the big picture, a life in transition for the Christian in view of her final destination.

The second idea, *exile*, conveys some similar notions under different imagery. Peter uses this terminology as well, referring to Christians as exiles scattered through various provinces (1 Pet 1:1), and as exiles living holy lives among pagans (1 Pet 1:11–12). Like a sojourner, an exile lives away from his true home. But while "sojourner" indicates that a person is unsettled and on the move, "exile" indicates that a person has been expelled from his own land. This image, too, is strikingly appropriate to describe Christians. At the beginning, God placed Adam and Eve in the sanctuary of the Garden of Eden, a place of intimate fellowship with God. But because of their fall, God expelled them from the Garden and consigned them to life east of Eden under his curse. The whole world as we know it is a place of exile. The good news of the gospel proclaims that God has rescued a people from fallen humanity and restored their place in his blessed presence—in fact, he has given them a place in his everlasting heavenly kingdom, a far better sanctuary than the Garden of Eden. But until Christ's return, Christians enjoy this fellowship with God in heaven only at a distance. Their time of exile remains for the time being, although they have a sure hope that God will soon bring it to an end.

Old Testament Israel's exile in Babylon is very important background for understanding why the New Testament describes Christians as exiles. Israel's experience was a kind of microcosm of the experience of the whole fallen human race. After so many centuries of Israelite disobedience, God sent King Nebuchadnezzar to destroy Jerusalem, to drive his people out of their Promised Land, and to haul them off into exile in Babylon. There God called them to live ordinary lives as far as possible—working, raising families, seeking the well-being of their foreign city—while they waited eagerly for God to end their exile and return them to their own land (see especially Jer 29:1–14). This, Peter suggests, is how Christians must live here and now. We do not await return to the earthly city of Jerusalem, but to what that earthly city represented: the "new Jerusalem" (Rev 21:2), the "Jerusalem that is above" (Gal 4:26). "If heaven is our country," John Calvin remarked, "what can earth be but a place of exile?"[8] Exiles should seek to live peaceful and productive lives in their foreign city, and sometimes can achieve great things in the city's affairs, as the example of Daniel and his friends well illustrates. But Scripture represents exile as *not* a place of glory. As we saw in Chapter 4, the departure of the pillar of cloud and fire from the temple presaged Israel's exile (Ezek 10), and the end of exile was marked by glory's return (Ezek 43; cf. Isa 40:3–5). Thus, Christians today ought to pursue peaceful and productive lives in their places of exile, while longing for the glory of the new creation.

A third and final biblical idea that helps us to understand the Christian's status in the present world is *dual citizenship*. Citizenship entails enjoying certain rights and privileges by association with a particular political polity. Christians, of course, are often citizens of an earthly nation (or nations), but Scripture identifies an even more important citizenship that they enjoy, thanks to Christ's redemptive work: citizenship in heaven. Consider Paul's example. He was a Roman citizen, a highly prized status that most inhabitants of the Roman Empire did not enjoy. Roman citizenship conferred certain legal privileges on Paul that he claimed when accused of wrongdoing (Acts 16:37–39; 22:23–29). But Paul taught that he, as a Christian, was also a citizen of another polity: "Our citizenship is in heaven" (Phil 3:20). He had *dual* citizenship.

On one hand, dual citizenship is a helpful notion to hold alongside our recognition that Christians are sojourners and exiles, because it reminds us that we should not take an entirely negative view of our lives in earthly cities and societies. Unlike these other two ideas, citizenship communicates a real sense of belonging and ordinarily instills an element of allegiance. In fact, we may feel a bit uneasy in saying that we are *both* sojourners/exiles in earthly communities *and* citizens within them, but this tension is surely what Scripture wants us to feel. Citizenship in an earthly country, and with it a modest patriotism, is not inconsistent with Christian profession. But love for our earthly country must be tempered by a much stronger devotion to our heavenly country.

Reading Paul leaves us with little doubt which of his citizenships conferred the greater benefits and instilled the higher loyalties. Roman citizenship saved Paul from a flogging in Acts 22—not a benefit I would

---

8. Calvin, *Institutes*, 3.9.4.

refuse—but that can hardly compare with being blessed "in the heavenly realms with every spiritual blessing in Christ" (Eph 1:3). The author of Hebrews promotes a similar perspective: "Here we do not have an enduring city, but we are looking for the city that is to come" (Heb 13:14). It's not that we don't belong at all to any city on earth. But what we do not have here is an *enduring* city. The city to come thus claims our ultimate allegiance. Paul's opening words in Colossians 3 are worth remembering: "Since, then, you have been raised with Christ, set your hearts on things above, where Christ is, seated at the right hand of God. Set your minds on things above, not on earthly things. For you died, and your life is now hidden with Christ in God. When Christ, who is your life, appears, then you also will appear with him in glory" (Col 3:1–4). And so we see again this familiar theme. The present world, with its earthly citizenships, is not a place of glory. Glory belongs to the heavenly city, where our Savior is, and therefore, where our true life is even now.

Glorifying God in This Present Evil Age

The preceding section attempted to portray a faithful biblical picture of this "present age"—that is, this world in which Christians have always lived, in distinction from the age to come, the glorious new creation. It is an evil age, yet God fills it with many good gifts; Christians, as sojourners, exiles, and dual citizens, can usually survive, and sometimes even thrive, within earthly communities, but their true home is Christ's heavenly kingdom of the age to come. In comparison to the age to come, the present age is not one of glory. What sort of life, then, is especially fitting for Christians in the midst of the decay around them, surrounded by things that are "temporary" (2 Cor 4:18) and "passing away" (1 Cor 7:31)? How do we bring glory to God in a non-glorious age?

Glorifying God in this present age means, first of all, to render right worship to him, especially in the church's corporate assembly. Previous chapters offered many biblical reasons why this is true, but perhaps most important here is the fact that our worship on earth is a participation in and a foretaste of that glory the angels and saints give to God in heaven. Our worship reveals a glimpse of the age to come even here in our humble Sunday gatherings.

The angels in heaven now cry out, "Amen! Praise and glory and wisdom and thanks and honor and power and strength be to our God for ever and ever. Amen!" (Rev 7:12). The saints who have entered heaven before us add to the angels' praise: "Great and marvelous are your deeds, Lord God Almighty. Just and true are your ways, King of the nations. Who will not fear you, Lord, and bring glory to your name?" (Rev 15:3–4). When God calls us to give him glory in worship—"Sing to the LORD a new song; sing to the LORD, all the earth. Sing to the LORD, praise his name; proclaim his salvation day after day. Declare his glory among the nations, his marvelous deeds among all peoples" (Ps 96:1–3)—he allows us to echo on earth what these angels and saints proclaim in heaven. Scripture even describes a kind of trafficking between earthly and heavenly worship. In our worship, we exhort the heavenly angels to render their worship: "Praise the LORD, you his angels, you mighty ones who do his bidding, who obey his word. Praise the LORD, all his heavenly hosts, you his servants who do his will" (Ps 103:20–21). And we don't just call out to these angels from a distance. In our worship, we "have come to Mount Zion, to the city of the living God, the heavenly Jerusalem," to the many thousands of angels, to the spirits of the departed saints—to Jesus himself (Heb 12:22–24). We participate mysteriously in the worship of heaven as we worship here on earth. In this activity, above all, we show forth the glory of God—the glory of the age to come—here in this present age.

As we also considered in previous chapters, our glorifying God in worship ought to radiate, secondarily, into all we do. "Each of you," Peter explains, "should use whatever gift you have received to serve others, as faithful stewards of God's grace in its various forms." Whether in speaking or serving, we do so "with the strength God provides, so that in all things God may be praised [glorified] through Jesus Christ. To him be the glory and the power for ever and ever" (1 Pet 4:10–11). We are called to serve. We surely don't give enough thought to the fact that God desires every Christian to put his gifts to use in service to his neighbor. Rather than looking at this call to service as a burden, we should rejoice that God is glorified through Christ as we roll up our sleeves and love one another.

If God should be glorified in *all* we do, as Peter says, it would take a comprehensive study of Christian ethics to describe how we glorify God here and now. I cannot do that in the few pages that remain, so I wish to focus upon the way we're called to live *in light of the passing nature of this present age*—that is, in light of the fact that this present age is not glorious. This was, in fact, precisely where Peter's thoughts turned after the words quoted above. "Dear friends," he continued, "do not be surprised at the fiery ordeal that has come on you to test you, as though something strange were happening to you. But rejoice inasmuch as you participate in the sufferings of Christ, so that you may be overjoyed when his glory is revealed" (1 Pet 4:12–13). Despite the many temporal and spiritual goods we already enjoy, this present age for Christians is a life under the cross, characterized by sufferings of various kinds, calling for *self-denial*, *patient endurance*, and steadfastly *waiting upon the Lord*. Only with these do we glorify God in all things.

Self-Denial

The idea of *self-denial* is rooted especially in Jesus' words from Matthew 16:24: "Whoever wishes to come after me, let him deny himself, and take up his cross, and follow me."[9] We don't seem to hear much today about self-denial in the Christian life. This is hardly surprising, since self-denial is about the last thing that comes naturally to us. In Matthew 16, Peter rebukes Jesus for saying that he must suffer many things in Jerusalem, be killed, and then rise to life (Matt 16:21–22). Jesus replies to Peter: "Get behind me, Satan! You are a stumbling block to me; you do not have in mind the concerns of God, but merely human concerns" (Matt 16:23). Human beings instinctively find God's way of salvation appalling: suffering first, and *then* glory. Christ himself "did not come to be served, but to serve, and to give his life as a ransom for many" (Mark 10:45), and Christians must follow the same pattern, though it's against our natural grain. Hence the need for self-denial. This is not a self-hatred, or a denial of our worth in God's sight, but a denial of all of those persistent sinful inclinations to resist God's will and selfishly serve ourselves.

Some of the strongest biblical exhortations to self-denial explain this obligation in light of the *glory to come*. After commanding self-denial in the text just considered, Jesus reasons with his disciples that the one who wants to save his life will lose it, but the one who loses his life for him will find it (Matt 16:25). Seeking one's glory in this age, in other words, leads to death. But "the Son of Man is going to come in his Father's glory with his angels, and then he will reward each person according to what [he has] done" (Matt 16:27). Glory belongs to the age to come, manifest at Christ's return. In the spirit of self-denial, therefore, we should not store up for ourselves perishable treasures on earth, but incorruptible treasures in heaven (Matt 6:19–20); we seek first God's kingdom and his righteousness (Matt 6:33).

Titus 2:11–13 brings together similar themes: "For the grace of God has appeared that offers salvation to all people. It teaches us to say 'No' to

---

9.   My own translation.

ungodliness and worldly passions, and to live self-controlled, upright and godly lives in this present age, while we wait for the blessed hope—the appearing of the glory of our great God and Savior, Jesus Christ." Saying "No" to ungodliness and worldly passions seems to be the same thing as Jesus' command to deny oneself. It is not self-hatred, but resisting those evil desires that stand contrary to God's will. Paul associates this ungodliness and worldly passion with *this present age*—what he calls elsewhere this present *evil* age (Gal 1:4). In contrast, he points to the coming age of Christ's return: "the appearing of the *glory* of our great God and Savior, Jesus Christ" (Titus 2:13). Faithful life in this present evil age, with a view to the glory to come, requires self-denial.

Although we don't hear much about self-denial in contemporary discussion of the Christian life, the Reformers and their Reformed heirs recognized its importance. Wilhelmus à Brakel provided this helpful definition: "Self-denial is a Christian virtue, granted by God to His children, whereby they, out of love for God's will, neither give heed nor yield to their intellect, will, and inclinations insofar as they are in opposition to the will of God—and oppose and suppress them instead. They do so by a voluntary forsaking and rejection of all that pertains to their natural well-being, if God's cause demands such from them—this is to the honor of God and the welfare of their neighbors."[10]

This reinforces the point above that we must deny ourselves specifically with respect to that which stands against God's will. Self-denial doesn't despise the well-being of one's soul, à Brakel adds shortly thereafter, but denies one's "*sinful* self," the "old Adam."[11] Consider also the end of his definition: self-denial is unto the honor (or *glory*) of God and the welfare of one's neighbors. Directly contrary to the narcissism considered in the previous chapter and rampant in contemporary culture, self-denial resists those persistent impulses that declare: it's all about *me*. How fitting that à Brakel comments: "A person who does not deny self shows that he is not satisfied unless everything ends in him."[12] This sums it up well. A narcissist lives for himself, indulging the desires of this present evil age. The one who fears and glorifies God denies himself and takes up his cross in light of the age to come.

---

10. à Brakel, *The Christian's Reasonable Service*, 3.397. (original italics removed)
11. Ibid., 3.399–400 (italics his)
12. Ibid., 3.405.

Calvin on Self-Denial

Perhaps no Reformed theologian has written as powerfully on self-denial as John Calvin, particularly in Book Three of *Institutes of the Christian Religion*. Early in his discussion of self-denial, Calvin recognizes the importance of Christians turning their eyes away from their own glory in this life: "When Scripture enjoins us to lay aside private regard to ourselves, it not only divests our minds of an excessive longing for wealth, or power, or human favor, but eradicates all ambition and thirst for worldly glory." Instead, Calvin reasons, Christians should view their lives as completely directed toward God. "For he who has learned to look to God in everything he does, is at the same time diverted from all vain thoughts. This is that self-denial which Christ so strongly enforces on his disciples from the very outset" (Matt 16:24).[13] Calvin certainly does not think this is easy. On the contrary, at times he seems almost overwhelmed by the difficulty of forsaking one's own glory and other self-centered attainments of the present life: "We have a frenzied desire, an infinite eagerness, to pursue wealth and honor, intrigue for power, accumulate riches, and collect all those frivolities which seem conducive to luxury and splendor."[14] The only person who "has properly denied himself," Calvin thus concludes, is the one "who has resigned himself entirely to the Lord, placing all the course of his life entirely at his disposal. . . . Whatever happens, knowing that it is ordered by the Lord, he will receive it with a placid and grateful mind."[15]

Calvin then turns specifically to Christ's teaching that to deny oneself, a person must take up his cross. He doesn't try to blunt the sobering power of Jesus' words: "Those whom the Lord has chosen and honored with his intercourse must prepare for a hard, laborious, troubled life, a life full of many and various kinds of evils." What comfort or strength is there, faced with these trials? Calvin turns his readers' minds to Christ, the glory he attained after suffering, and our share in that same glory: "Having begun this course with Christ the first-born, he continues it towards all his children. . . . Hence it affords us great consolation in hard and difficult circumstances . . . to think that we are holding fellowship with the sufferings of Christ; that as he passed to celestial glory through a labyrinth of many woes, so we too are conducted thither through various tribulations."[16] Calvin also reminds readers that God has many good

---

13. Calvin, *Institutes*, 3.7.2.
14. Ibid., 3.7.8.
15. Ibid., 3.9.10.
16. Ibid., 3.8.1.

purposes in bringing us to glory along the path of hardship and self-denial. The constant reminder of our weakness and frailty, for example, represses our stubborn arrogance and builds our patience.[17] And God consoles us with a wonderful thought when we're persecuted for righteousness' sake: "How high the honor which God bestows upon us in distinguishing us by the special badge of his soldiers."[18]

For Calvin, it seems fair to say, learning to bear the cross in a life of self-denial centers around meditation upon and desire for the future life of glory. He states, "Whatever be the kind of tribulation with which we are afflicted we should always consider the end of it to be, that we may be trained to despise the present, and thereby to aspire to the future life," and "We duly profit from the discipline of the cross, when we learn that this life, estimated in itself, is restless, troubled, in numberless ways wretched, and plainly in no respect happy."[19] These statements about the present life are bracing and may strike us as exaggerated. Calvin does offer important qualifications, noting that we should not hate the present life or be ungrateful to God for the many blessings he gives in it.[20] Still, Calvin truly did embrace the call of Paul and other biblical writers to heavenly-mindedness. Christ's kingdom, he explained, is not carnal or earthly but spiritual and heavenly.[21] Thus, "the cross of Christ . . . only triumphs in the breasts of believers over the devil and the flesh, sin and sinners, when their eyes are directed to the power of his resurrection."[22]

Patient Endurance

True self-denial through the trials of life, nourished by the hope of everlasting glory, is accompanied by *patient endurance*. À Brakel defines patience as "the believer's spiritual strength which he has in God whereby he, in the performance of his duty, willingly, with composure, joyfully, and steadfastly endures all the vicissitudes of life, having a hope that the outcome will be well."[23]

On one hand, self-denial *requires* patient endurance. It is difficult enough to deny one's selfish, God-displeasing inclinations for a short time, but to do so more and more over a lifetime demands precisely the sort

17. Ibid., 3.8.2, 4.
18. Ibid., 3.8.7.
19. Ibid., 3.9.1.
20. Ibid., 3.9.3.
21. Ibid., 2.15.4.
22. Ibid., 3.9.6.
23. à Brakel, *The Christian's Reasonable Service*, 3.413 (original italics removed).

of strength of character we associate with patience. On the other hand, self-denial *fosters* the development of patient endurance.[24] Paul says that "suffering produces perseverance" (Rom 5:3), and James writes that "the testing of your faith produces perseverance" (Jas 1:3). Of course, they do not mean that suffering or testing *automatically* engenders perseverance, regardless of our response to it. Rather, suffering and trial call forth self-denial (indeed, self-denial is hardly necessary when there's no temptation to face), and self-denial calls forth perseverance (again, perseverance is hardly necessary when there's no demand for self-denial over an extended period). To put it another way, the Holy Spirit builds patient endurance in believers as they practice self-denial over a lifetime of trials. A person cannot grow in one without growing in the other. "All those who are now bearers of the crown have been bearers of the cross. . . . Consider that the way to heaven is the way of affliction, and that we cannot walk upon this way except by way of patience."[25]

Hope

Patient endurance is intimately connected to *hope*. This is hardly surprising, since heavenly-mindedness is necessary for self-denial. As meditation on the future life sustains self-denial, so hope undergirds patience. Hence Paul commends the Thessalonian Christians for their "endurance inspired by hope in our Lord Jesus Christ" (1 Thess 1:3). As à Brakel puts it, "there is much time, much cross-bearing, and much strife between promise and possession. Then hope comes and shows the glory of the benefits and the certainty of becoming a partaker of them. This is followed by patience, which supports hope so that it does not succumb due to tribulations."[26] As self-denial and patient endurance are mutually reinforcing, so apparently are hope and patient endurance. Paul speaks of "endurance inspired by hope" (1 Thess 1:3) and also writes that as suffering produces perseverance, so also "perseverance [produces] character; and character, hope" (Rom 5:3–4). In what, precisely, do we hope? Paul explains in the same context: "We boast in the hope of the glory of God" (Rom 5:2). Thus, we see again the theme of this chapter: setting our eyes upon God's glory entails a longing for the age to come and steadfastness in the face of present trials.

---

24. Ibid., 3.413.
25. Ibid., 3.425.
26. Ibid., 3.324.

Joy and Courage

Many other virtues may come to mind as we reflect on this hopeful perseverance, but I mention two more that urge us to maintain a positive focus and to engage actively in the affairs of this world: *joy* and *courage*. Attention to themes such as self-denial and patient endurance, although necessary, may suggest that the Christian life is simply one of grim resignation. Joy and courage, however, should keep this temptation at bay.

Joy is not easy to define. It is easily confused with happiness, but that is surely incorrect. Happiness is a mood or feeling that people experience more or less in different times and circumstances. Christian joy, however, is a deep-seated virtue of the heart, not a mood that waxes and wanes. I take joy, in brief, to refer to a delight in God, in his good gifts, and in our vocation to serve him.

One of the ways we can see most poignantly the difference between happiness and joy is Scripture's emphasis that joy emerges through suffering, and even that we rejoice in our suffering. In contrast, suffering does not make anyone happy. No one likes suffering, and by definition we are unhappy about what we don't like. But Paul and James, in texts considered above, did associate suffering and joy. Paul says that "we rejoice in the hope of the glory of God, and not only this, but we also rejoice in afflictions, knowing that affliction produces perseverance" (Rom 5:2-3).[27] James opens his epistle with the exhortation: "Consider it pure joy, my brothers, whenever you face trials of many kinds" (Jas 1:2). These texts do not commend joy in suffering because we should take delight in the sufferings themselves. As I defined it above, joy is delight in God, his good gifts, and our vocation to serve him. Thus, joy itself, Paul explains, is rooted in our justification by faith and the peace and access we therefore have before God, and our hope of the coming glory of God (Rom 5:1-2).

Joy, like the other virtues we've been considering, is nourished by reflection on the glory of the age to come. Just before Paul makes his most famous statements about joy, early in Philippians 4, he reminds us that our citizenship is in heaven and that we await the resurrection of the body—the body of glory—at Christ's return (Phil 3:20–21). Immediately after his command to rejoice in the Lord always, he notes, "the Lord is near" (Phil 4:5). The author of Hebrews takes the same perspective when he encourages readers, faced with the entanglements of sin and the temptation to lose heart, to fix their "eyes on Jesus, the pioneer and perfecter of

---

27. My translation.

faith. For the joy set before him he endured the cross, scorning its shame, and sat down at the right hand of the throne of God" (Heb 12:1–3). It is Christ and the glory we will one day share with him that delights us in the midst of present sufferings. Yet there is also a sense in which we rejoice *in* these sufferings. Again, this is not because we delight in hardship for its own sake, as if it is an end in itself. Instead, both Paul and James explain, we rejoice in sufferings because it is precisely through suffering that God builds various virtues in us, such as perseverance and hope, which make us "mature and complete" (Jas 1:3–4; Rom 5:3–4).

As joy fosters a positive delight in God even while we practice self-denial, so likewise *courage* fosters a spirit of service to God and neighbor even while we patiently endure the hardships that buffet us. Courage refers to the strength to stand fast and to carry out our responsibilities in the face of fear and opposition. Far from drawing upon a stoic indifference to the evils around us, courage is only courage when we feel the weight of hardships that assault us and threaten our well-being. Courage does not pretend there's no danger, but stands firm before it in the fear of God. Thus, á Brakel explains the need for courage: "Not only does much time elapse between the promise and the possession of the matter which hope assuredly anticipates, but also much opposition from enemies is to be expected. Therefore, the person who exercises hope needs to be valiant in order to endure all things and overcome all obstacles."[28]

Self-denial and hope require patient endurance, but patient endurance is not about cowering in a corner and killing time until the storm passes. Until Christ comes, God wants us to love him with all of our heart, soul, mind, and strength. He calls us to love our neighbors as ourselves. Proclaiming the gospel, standing with the church, promoting the cause of righteousness, and any other service that defends God's truth inevitably provokes opposition. Whole-hearted devotion to Christ is not the easy way out in this present age. But those who fear God need not fear fellow humans: "Do not be afraid of those who kill the body but cannot kill the soul. Rather, be afraid of the One who can destroy both soul and body in hell. Are not two sparrows sold for a penny? Yet not one of them will fall to the ground outside your Father's care. And even the very hairs of your head are all numbered. So don't be afraid; you are worth more than many sparrows" (Matt 10:28–31). In fact, those who belong to Christ may be courageous in the face of every opponent in this present evil age:

---

28. á Brakel, *The Christian's Reasonable Service*, 3.324.

"Neither death nor life, neither angels nor demons, neither the present nor the future, nor any powers, neither height nor depth, nor anything else in all creation, will be able to separate us from the love of God that is in Christ Jesus our Lord" (Rom 8:38–39).

Waiting upon the Lord

There is probably no single virtue or activity that can satisfactorily sum up the way of glorifying God in this present age, in eager anticipation of the glory to come. But I close by mentioning something that, like self-denial, receives far too little attention in contemporary discussions of the Christian life: *waiting upon the Lord.* God has promised his people a breathtaking restoration from exile, along a superhighway in the wilderness made straight and level for the Messiah himself, through which "the glory of the LORD will be revealed, and all people will see it together" (Isa 40:3–5). But exile is hard, and restoration from exile does not come right away. Thus, God calls his people to *wait*: "They that wait upon the LORD shall renew their strength; they shall mount up with wings as eagles; they shall run, and not be weary; and they shall walk, and not faint" (Isa 40:31).[29] Biblical waiting is not the kind of bored waiting that we do while sitting at the DMV or holding on the phone for customer service. It is a waiting of self-denial, of the hope of glory, and of active service. Paul brings these themes together so harmoniously in a text mentioned above: "For the grace of God has appeared that offers salvation to all people. It teaches us to say 'No' to ungodliness and worldly passions, and to live self-controlled, upright and godly lives in this present age, while we wait for the blessed hope—the appearing of the glory of our great God and Savior, Jesus Christ, who gave himself for us to redeem us from all wickedness and to purify for himself a people that are his very own, eager to do what is good" (Titus 2:11–14).

Conclusion

Scripture describes this present age as one that is not glorious. This is true in a relative rather than absolute sense. In comparison with the glory of the age to come, this present age, passing away and pervaded by sin, has no glory. As sojourners and exiles in the world, Christians live as those who already belong to the coming age, placing no ultimate hope in the treasures

---

29. This familiar translation is from the King James Version.

and achievements of their earthly societies. Yet God calls us to live godly and productive lives. Thus may we, with self-denial, patient endurance, and a host of Spirit-wrought virtue, glorify God in our worship and faithful obedience in all of our callings, while we wait eagerly for the great day of the Lord to be revealed.

Soli Deo gloria. No merely human book can ever hope to capture sufficiently the brilliance and depth of this theme. But it is well worth the effort to reflect anew on this life-changing idea that animated the Reformation and has inspired countless believers ever since. Truly, "Glory to God Alone" is the majestic heart of Christian faith and life.

To explore this grand theme, we have focused upon a particular story-line in Scripture, and while it does not capture comprehensively everything Scripture teaches, this storyline traces the revelation of God's glory through many of the key events in biblical history. God revealed his glory in the pillar of cloud and fire in the wilderness when the Israelites came out of Egypt. This cloud settled on Sinai and on their portable tabernacle, it led them to the Promised Land, and finally settled on the temple in Jerusalem. Revealed as the presence of God with his people, the cloud was simultaneously a great blessing and source of terror, for the holy glory of God could not abide with a persistently sinful people. The story of God's glory seemed as though it might come to a tragic end when the cloud departed from the temple and Babylon hauled the remnant of Judah off into exile.

But God in his gracious wisdom was not finished with his people. He restored them to the Promised Land and they rebuilt their temple. Yet his magnificent promises about the glory to come was never—and could never have been—fulfilled in an earthly temple in the small land of Palestine. In the fullness of time, God sent forth his Son, the promised Messiah, who came in the glory of the Spirit and brings all of God's promises to consummation. Although his glory was veiled during the humiliation of his earthly ministry and horrible death at Calvary, God has raised him in glory and seated him—a human being in our own flesh and blood—at his right hand in the majesty of the new creation. From there, he ministers on our behalf from the heavenly temple and pours out his Spirit to apply to us all the benefits of his redeeming work. Now there remains but one great event, the second coming of our great Lord, who will appear not in the humility of his first coming, but in a cloud of glory to judge the living and the dead and to welcome his children into the glory of his Father.

This storyline confirms one of the great insights of the Reformation and later Reformed theologians: first and foremost, God glorifies *himself,* but he glorifies himself in part through glorifying us and allowing us to glorify him through our godly response to his grace. Over and against the temptation in some contemporary quarters to make *soli Deo gloria* primarily about our own projects for glorifying God, and thus ironically about *us*, Scripture calls us back to affirm that *soli Deo gloria* is truly about *God*. Yet what a high privilege we enjoy in that God is pleased to glorify himself through the salvation of poor sinners and to make us instruments of the manifestation of the glory that belongs to him alone.

May God glorify himself in all of his works. May our thoughts and worship revel in the glory of the living God even in the midst of an age of distraction and narcissism. And may we, the undeserving but ever-blessed beneficiaries of such a great salvation, live for his glory now as we wait for the dawning of that day when he glorifies us together with his Son.

Select Bibliography

Bavinck, Herman. *Reformed Dogmatics*, vol. 2, *God and Creation*. Edited by John Bolt. Translated by John Vriend. Grand Rapids: Baker Academic, 2004.

_____. *Reformed Dogmatics*. Vol. 3: *Sin and Salvation in Christ*. Edited by John Bolt. Translated by John Vriend. Grand Rapids: Baker Academic, 2006.

Beale, G, K. *A New Testament Biblical Theology: The Unfolding of the Old Testament in the New*. Grand Rapids: Baker Academic, 2011.

_____. *The Temple and the Church's Mission: A Biblical Theology of the Dwelling Place of God*. Downers Grove, IL: InterVarsity Press, 2004.

Brakel, Wilhelmus à. *The Christian's Reasonable Service*. Vol. 3. Translated by Bartel Elshout. Pittsburgh: Soli Deo Gloria, 1994.

Bullinger, Henry. *The Decades of Henry Bullinger, The Fourth Decade*. Edited by Thomas Harding. Cambridge: Cambridge University Press, 1851.

Calvin, John. *Institutes of the Christian Religion*. Translated by Henry Beveridge. Grand Rapids: Eerdmans, 1953.

_____. *Calvin's Commentaries*. Vol. 2.

_____. *Calvin's Commentaries*. Vol. 21. Grand Rapids: Baker, 2003.

_____. *Calvin's Commentaries*. Vol. 22. Grand Rapids: Baker, 1999.

Carr, Nicholas. *The Shallows: What the Internet Is Doing to Our Brains*. New York: Norton, 2010.

Challies, Tim. *The Next Story: Life and Faith After the Digital Explosion*. Grand Rapids: Zondervan, 2011.

DeYoung, Rebecca Konyndyk. *Glittering Vices: A New Look at the Seven Deadly Sins and Their Remedies*. Grand Rapids: Brazos, 2009.

DeYoung, Rebecca Konyndyk. *Vainglory: The Forgotten Vice*. Grand Rapids: Eerdmans, 2014.

"Edward Leigh," in *Dictionary of National Biography*. Vol. 32. Edited by Sidney Lee. New York: Macmillan, 1892.

Edwards, Jonathan. "The End for Which God Created the World," in *God's Passion for His Glory: Living the Vision of Jonathan Edwards*. Translated by John Piper. Wheaton, IL: Crossway, 1998.

Ferguson, Sinclair B. *The Holy Spirit*. Downers Grove, IL: InterVarsity Press, 1996.

Fesko, J. V. *The Theology of the Westminster Standards: Historical Context & Theological Insights*. Wheaton, IL: Crossway, 2014.

Hamilton, James M. *God's Glory in Salvation Through Judgment: A Biblical Theology*. Wheaton, IL: Crossway, 2010.

Hannah, John D. *Basics of the Reformed Faith Series:How Do We Glorify God?* Phillipsburg, NJ: P&R, 2008.

Jackson, Maggie. *Distracted: The Erosion of Attention and the Coming Dark Age.* Amherst, NY: Prometheus, 2008.

Johnson, Terry L. *The Case for Traditional Protestantism: The Solas of the Reformation.* Carlisle, PA: Banner of Truth, 2004.

Kelsey, Candice M. *Generation MySpace: Helping Your Teen Survive Online Adolescence.* New York: Marlowe, 2007.

Kline, Meredith G. *Images of the Spirit.* Grand Rapids: Baker, 1980.

Kristanto, Billy. *Sola Dei Gloria: The Glory of God in the Thought of John Calvin.* New York: Peter Lang, 2011.

Lasch, Christopher. *The Culture of Narcissism: American Life in an Age of Diminishing Expectations.* New York: Norton, 1978.

Leigh, Edward. *A Treatise of Divinity.* London, 1662.

Lohse, Bernhard. *Martin Luther's Theology: Its Historical and Systematic Development.* Translated by Roy A. Harrisville. Minneapolis: Fortress, 1999.

Luther, Martin. "Heidelberg Disputation." In *Luther's Works.* Vol. 31. Edited by Harold J. Grimm. Philadelphia: Fortress, 1957.

McGrath, Alister. *Luther's Theology of the Cross: Martin Luther's Theological Breakthrough.* Oxford: Basil Blackwell, 1985.

Milgrom, Jacob. *The JPS Torah Commentary: Numbers.* Philadelphia: Jewish Publication Society, 1990.

Muller, Richard A. *Post-Reformation Reformed Dogmatics: The Rise and Development of Reformed Orthodoxy, ca. 1520 to ca. 1725.* 4 vols. Grand Rapids: Baker Academic, 2003.

Murray, John. *Collected Writings.* Vol. 2. Carlisle, PA: Banner of Truth, 1977.

_____. *The Epistle to the Romans.* Vol. 1. Grand Rapids: Eerdmans, 1959.

_____. *Principles of Conduct: Aspects of Biblical Ethics.* Grand Rapids: Eerdmans, 1957.

_____. *Redemption: Accomplished and Applied.* Grand Rapids: Eerdmans, 1955.

Pelikan, Jaroslav. *Bach Among the Theologians.* Philadelphia: Fortress, 1986.

Piper, John. *God's Passion for His Glory: Living the Vision of Jonathan Edwards.* Wheaton, IL: Crossway, 1998.

Schreiner, Susan E. *The Theater of His Glory: Nature and the Natural Order in the Thought of John Calvin.* Durham: Labyrinth, 1991.

Schreiner, Thomas R. *The King in His Beauty: A Biblical Theology of the Old and New Testaments.* Grand Rapids: Baker Academic, 2013.

_____. *New Testament Theology: Magnifying God in Christ.* Grand Rapids: Baker Academic, 2008.

_____. *Paul: Apostle of God's Glory in Christ: A Pauline Theology.* Downers Grove, IL: InterVarsity Press, 2001.

Schultze, Quentin J. *Habits of the High-Tech Heart: Living Virtuously in the Information Age.* Grand Rapids: Baker Academic, 2002.

Sproul, R. C. Jr. *"Soli Deo Gloria"* in *After Darkness, Light: Distinctives of Reformed Theology: Essays in Honor of R. C. Sproul.* Edited by R. C. Sproul Jr. Phillipsburg, NJ: P&R, 2003.

Stapert, Calvin R. *My Only Comfort: Death, Deliverance, and Discipleship in the Music of Bach.* Grand Rapids: Eerdmans, 2000.

Steiner-Adair, Catherine. *The Big Disconnect: Protecting Childhood and Family Relationships in the Digital Age.* New York: HarperCollins, 2013.

Trueman, Carl R. and R. Scott Clark, eds. *Protestant Scholasticism: Essays in Reassessment.* Carlisle: Paternoster, 1999.

Twenge, Jean M. and W. Keith Campbell. *The Narcissism Epidemic: Living in the Age of Entitlement.* New York: Free Press, 2009.

Van Dixhoorn, Chad. *Confessing the Faith: A Reader's Guide to the Westminster Confession of Faith.* Carlisle, PA: Banner of Truth, 2014.

VanDrunen, David. *Divine Covenants and Moral Order: A Biblical Theology of Natural Law.* Grand Rapids: Eerdmans, 2014.

_____. *Living in God's Two Kingdoms: A Biblical Vision for Christianity and Culture.* Wheaton, IL: Crossway, 2010.

Vos, Geerhardus. *The Pauline Eschatology.* Grand Rapids: Eerdmans, 1972.

Witsius, Herman. *Sacred Dissertations on the Lord's Prayer.* Translated by William Pringle. Escondido, CA: The den Dulk Christian Foundation, 1994.

Young, Davis A. *John Calvin and the Natural World.* Lanham, MD: University Press of America, 2007.

Scripture Index

Subject Index

THE 5 SOLAS SERIES

Faith Alone — The Doctrine of Justification

What the Reformers Taught…
and Why It Still Matters

*Thomas Schreiner; Matthew Barrett,
Series Editor*

Historians and theologians have long recognized that at the heart of the sixteenth-century Protestant Reformation were five declarations, often referred to as the "solas:: sola scriptura, solus Christus, sola gratia, sola fide, and soli Deo gloria. These five statements summarize much of what the Reformation was about, and they distinguish Protestantism from other expressions of the Christian faith. Protestants place ultimate and final authority in the Scriptures, acknowledge the work of Christ alone as sufficient for redemption, recognize that salvation is by grace alone through faith alone, and seek to do all things for God's glory.

In *Faith Alone — The Doctrine of Justification* biblical scholar Thomas Schreiner looks at the historical and biblical roots of the doctrine of justification. He summarizes the history of the doctrine, looking at the early church and the writings of several of the Reformers. Then, he turns his attention to the Scriptures and walks readers through an examination of the key texts in the Old and New Testament. He discusses whether justification is transformative or forensic and introduces readers to some of the contemporary challenges to the Reformation teaching of sola fide, with particular attention to the new perspective on Paul.

Available in stores and online!